Since the terror attacks of September 11th, 2001, many books have been written by eyewitnesses, broadcasters, and victims' families, detailing several perspectives on that horrible day. But Jim Jenkins invites us to look at those events, and many others, with a new perspective. As a military chaplain at Ground Zero, Jenkins writes with keen insight, sharing personal stories and a spiritual perspective that invites us to see the tragedy in the context of history, our nation, and God's plan for the world. Each chapter is fascinating as we come face to face with many of the first responders, shovel operators, Red Cross workers, rescue dogs, and even the Mayor of New York at the time, Rudy Giuliani. You'll become immediately engrossed with the human stories but even more, you'll feel the hope of God as Jenkins allows Him to lead us through this dark tunnel of history into the light of His glory. Some of the stories are difficult to read, but each one leaves readers with the hope and encouragement that God is still on the throne and that He has a beautiful plan for each of our lives.

— SANDY SILVERTHORNE, PASTOR AND
AWARD-WINNING AUTHOR

For those who responded to Ground Zero, Jim Jenkins' words do a very delicate job of bringing back the sights, the sounds, the smells—and yes, the darkness—of the experience. This book gives the reader an inside view into the experience of serving at the hallowed ground of 9/11. Jim does this while weaving in the reassurance that none of us were alone. God, the Holy Spirit, was and always is with us.

Jim vows to never let people forget what happened on September 11th, 2001, and *From Rubble to Redemption* will help keep that vow. Thank you, Jim, for sharing not only your experiences, but your personal vulnerabilities that have resulted from your service.

— ANNE HUMPHREYS (BYBEE) WILLIAMS, GROUND ZERO LOGISTICS EXPERT, NDMS MISSION SUPPORT TEAM, AND PHOTOGRAPHER OF "THE CROSS AT GROUND ZERO"

Dr. Jim Jenkins has given us an in-depth, up-close-and-personal account of the 9/11 recovery effort at Ground Zero. *From Rubble to Redemption* is very informative and thought-provoking, shocking us with tragic incidents of grief, yet healing us with hope-giving biblical perspectives. This reminder of America's worst national tragedy to date is a healthy tonic. And it's very timely: If Americans—especially Christians—do not awaken to righteousness, another wake-up call, far worse, is coming.

— GREG HINNANT, PROFESSOR,
CHRISTIAN LIFE SCHOOL OF THEOLOGY
GLOBAL

FROM RUBBLE TO REDEMPTION

A Ground Zero Chaplain Remembers

JIM JENKINS

CALLED WRITERS
CHRISTIAN PUBLISHING

COPYRIGHT

Published by Called Writers Christian Publishing, LLC

Tuscaloosa, Alabama

Print version ISBN: 978-1-7354760-4-9

DEDICATION

The word 'dedication' has to do with something, or someone, set apart for a sacred purpose.
I would like to dedicate this book to a few people who represent the thousands that stepped up to help on 9/11. From the dump truck drivers who hauled away the rubble of World Trade Center 24/7, to scores of volunteers who sifted through the debris looking for human remains, to the people of Gander Newfoundland, who opened their homes and their hearts to strangers whose flights were diverted there. Everyone had a purpose—I believe a God-ordained purpose.

This is Anne (Bybee) Williams. She was tasked with coordinating logistical support at Ground Zero. One day while walking through the Pile, she grabbed a disposable camera and took the photo that serves as the cover of

my book. She graciously gave permission to use what I believe is a historic treasure: "The Cross in the Pile." Like so many dedicated professionals she provided enormously significant support to the huge recovery operation.

These 2 women traveled from Oregon to Ground Zero with their specially trained dogs. On the left is Pat Gartman and her dog, whose name you will learn later in this book. On the right is  *Cindy Ehlers and her dog, Tikvah. In Hebrew, Tikvah means 'hope.' That is exactly what these two women and their remarkable dogs brought to Ground Zero. Hope to the families that their loved ones might be found in the Pile. Hope to those searching that their labors were not in vain. Hope to the Morgue workers and other first responders who were 'dog-tired' (pun intended) and needed the comfort these noble animals provided.*

CONTENTS

FOREWORD

Being a United States Air Force Veteran, and a law enforcement officer for over 25 years, I can tell you that Dr. Jenkins nails it in this book. He so clearly describes what a person goes through when they suffer a traumatic event, and how important it is to recognize the struggle and seek help. During my time as a police officer, I have attended countless Critical Incident debriefings, and Dr. Jenkins has presided over several of them. He has had an amazing career as a Navy Chaplain and as a Pastor.

This book will take you through nearly every emotion. It will make you smile. It will make you weep.

And you will feel the anguish as if you were there at Ground Zero witnessing these events for yourself. Most importantly, if you understand the intent, this book will bring you great joy and hope in the end.

Dr. Jenkins not only touches on the aftermath of 9/11, but also the current events that are tearing this country apart. He makes a very convincing case that what is happening right now is not ultimately political, racial, anti-police, or anything else that can be explained strictly in natural terms. Rather, there is an unseen spiritual war taking place, and the one behind that war is using race, politics, and a worldwide pandemic as tools to divide us.

We have an enemy that wants to destroy what was created to be a place of freedom: freedom of speech, freedom of religion, and everything thing else that our forefathers intended this country to be. You might think that you cannot see this spiritual war, but you can see very clearly the effects of it.

Wrong has now become right. Compassion and patience for our fellow man seems to be a thing of the past. We appear to be headed down a very dark road.

Fortunately, Dr. Jenkins doesn't leave us stranded in a sea of despair. Instead, he points us to the very simple solution to these problems.

Read this book with an open mind and you will find the Truth, "and the Truth will set you free."

— STEVEN C. TIMM, UNITED STATES AIR
FORCE VETERAN, LAW ENFORCEMENT
OFFICER, AND TWO-TIME MEDAL OF
VALOR RECIPIENT

INTRODUCTION

The geese in the distance were honking their intention to get back up north.

As I write this, it's 2021 and the ice storm in Oregon is over. Some of the more odious pandemic restrictions are being eased—just enough to hint at some sense of normalcy after a nightmarish year of lockdowns, wildfires, and non-stop riots in the streets.

While driving on the interstate, I started to notice a pattern. Every few minutes a crumpled up, letter-sized piece of paper hit my windshield. One sheet, then another. After passing a few cars, I spotted the culprit. It was a garbage truck. For some reason it was only letter-sized missives that were hitting my Jeep.

In an instant my mind went back to September 11th, 2001. As the nation was shocked by the events of that day, one memory that sticks out in mind is the sight of millions of pieces of paper wafting down like lake-effect snow as the fires raged and the jumpers fell. The World Trade Center after all, was all about papers—documents, notarized appraisals, faxes, memos.

As I concentrated on my driving, hoping one of those papers wouldn't stick to my windshield and impede my vision, I thought back to the streets of Manhattan which had been blanketed by a carpet of papers soaked in jet fuel. Was there a signed contract for a million-dollar investment deal? Was there a termination letter from someone cleaning out his desk when the plane hit? Was there a printed email that was in the process of translation? Was there a Post-it note reading: "call home"? Was there a crayon drawing from a grandchild, or a menu from the Windows on The World restaurant?

As I drove on, I think it was the steady, almost rhythmic release of one page after another that got my attention. I was after all in the final stages of writing the book you are about to read. Writing it has been a process of one page, one memory at a time, spanning the last two decades. And there was always the wondering. What was the message being broadcast to humanity from the garbage trucks that hauled debris out of Ground Zero?

A pastor friend of mine asked me early on, "So how will you approach a book about your time at Ground Zero after 20 years have gone by?" Almost without hesitation, I said "It's going to be about rubble. I'm going to follow the rubble, address the reality of the rubble, its long-term effects, and its prophetic significance."

As I continued my drive north, I was getting closer to Portland—the site of some of the most violent protests of the summer of 2020. I couldn't believe my eyes. The signs and billboards were defaced and covered with graffiti. Blue tarps and garbage littered the shoulder of the road.

I had not driven north since the riots and I never imagined that kind of destruction would be allowed to take place on an interstate highway. Perhaps most shocking of all to me was the fact that the "artwork" was not the product of some loner tagging a billboard with a spray can. These were huge letters that took a lot of time and effort to produce. Either cherry pickers were used to lift the Antifa artist into place for a lengthy period of time, or they were lowered by a harness long enough to produce these colossal eyesores. Two things were abundantly clear to me in that moment. First, the police must have been told to stand down and not interfere with what was taking place. Second, the city was making no effort to clean up the mess even months later.

Homeless camps are springing up everywhere. Once beautiful areas are now reduced to burned-out, desolate debris fields. America is being torn down. In a matter of a few months, the whole world, it seems, has been shaken. To quote the prophet, "Truth is trampled in the streets."

On the twentieth anniversary of the last time we went through something like this, I write to remind us how it felt to wake up to scenes of horrific destruction, burning rubble and non-stop "fasten your seatbelt" warnings. If 9/11 was a wake-up call, then 2021 is a global trumpet blast.

This is a book about God. This is a book about us. And finally, this is a book about our children and our grandchildren. In a mere 20 years, the impact and the significance of the events of September 11th have been blunted, distorted, and co-opted by those who wish to dismantle all that we once held dear.

I believe that we are experiencing events of biblical

proportions, and we would do well to look to God's Word for the truth.

My earnest prayer is that you will not only see things through the lens of God's Word, but that you will be drawn to seek the face of God, the only constant in this turbulent time. I have done my best to accurately report what I saw, and what I feel the Lord spoke to me. My memories, like the pieces of paper hitting my windshield, are sometimes crumpled up. I have done my best to unravel them and relay them to you for your consideration.

To God be the glory.

PAST IS PROLOGUE

THE STENCH of death hung in the air like a miasma from some hellish swamp. At the end of the block was a wall of bare plywood. The wall had been erected to hide the fleet of refrigerator trucks which were filled with small frozen parcels.

No matter how much the Medical Examiner's staff tried to show appropriate reverence and respect, it still boiled down to a grisly scene. A gowned masked worker would be dispatched to a refrigerator truck. He would then bring one of the frozen parcels to exhausted forensic workers who, in assembly-line fashion, were examining them in tents to try and retrieve some clues about who and what they were dealing with.

Our team of chaplains closed out the last third of each day at the largest indoor space I had ever seen—a pier building that housed all the agencies investigating the worst crime scene in American history, as well as those who were coordinating all the services to surviving family members.

One image periodically still crashes into my mind all

these years later—a draped-off area that served as a giant nursery and childcare area for all the kids who lost parents in the collapse of the Twin Towers. The size of the place and the number of kids being cared for there were stunning. It was larger than the size of the sanctuary of the church I had pastored back in Oregon. During my time at Ground Zero, the number of kids I saw in that draped-off area was higher than the headcount of my full congregation back in Oregon—about 300 at the time.

I described the scene as if it happened yesterday. The radio show host sat silent, listening respectfully. Listeners who had called in before me were anything but respectful.

Driving along Interstate 5 from Oregon to California, I had tuned into KGO, a radio station from San Francisco that has a monster signal. As soon as I crossed their frequency, the show caught my attention. They were talking about the so-called "Ground Zero Mosque."

We were near the 10th anniversary of 9/11, and controversy had arisen surrounding a proposed Islamic Cultural Center to be constructed a few short blocks from Ground Zero. This 13-story Islamic Community Center and Place of Prayer, as described by the developers, was to be erected on the site where the former building had been condemned. The condemned building was damaged by the collapse of the Twin Towers, so the proposed Islamic center felt like a huge slap in the face to many people. Though the development was officially called Park51, it became known as "the Ground Zero Mosque."

The host of the radio show was soliciting callers to weigh in on the heated issue.

The longer I listened to this show, the angrier I got. Every single caller was repeating various talking points about diversity and inclusion. Not one person mentioned the people of New York or anyone who had personally lived through the nightmare of 9/11.

Pulling over to the shoulder, I hurriedly dialed the number to KGO. Over and over I dialed until I finally got to the call screener, all the while hoping that the 18-wheelers whizzing by me were being driven by people who had gotten plenty of sleep the night before.

As I waited to go on the air, I prayed that God would help me curb my tongue, stay on point, and address the heart of the matter. By that time, I had been a pastor for almost thirty years. For twenty of those years, I had served as a Navy Chaplain (Reserve), and in that capacity, I had been deployed to Ground Zero on September 23rd, 2001.

I started by giving the radio listeners a brief overview of our daily schedule. I spent a third of each day at the actual site of the collapsed Twin Towers, with those who were searching for human remains. The site was still on fire and periodically, flumes of fire would spout upward like geysers.

The next third of each day I spent at the little tent city attached to the Medical Examiner's office . . . the Morgue. After describing the scene at the Morgue, I realized the host was not going to interrupt me. I could say whatever was on my heart, unimpeded. I continued:

I've been listening for half an hour and no one has even brought up the families who populated that nursery in New York. The first responders. The now pre-teens whose lives were forever changed. Many of the callers have mentioned the beauty of Islam. Others have criticized the narrow-minded Islamophobes. But nobody has mentioned Sal.

Sal is the excavator operator who climbed into his rig day after day and dug his huge yellow claw into the rubble before shaking it out in the hope of retrieving human remains. I spoke to Sal every day, and one day it just occurred to me to ask him a question.

Pointing toward the chasm all around us, I spoke up, "Sal, I never thought to ask—do you have someone?"

As I directed my eyes to the smoking rubble, he quietly turned his hard hat around and then showed me two pictures —his brother and his brother's son. They had both been firefighters, and now they were buried in the mass of rubble.

I continued sharing my perspective with the talk show audience.

You've all spoken so clinically and theoretically about geopolitics and a utopian vision of harmony, but I haven't heard anyone discuss PTSD. I haven't heard anyone mention how triggers can bring back all of the horrors in a nanosecond.

By this time, sitting there on the side of Interstate 5, I was experiencing that exact phenomenon—I could smell the stench of decomposing bodies as if it were 2001 all over again. PTSD is like that. Sometimes the mere rehearsal of an event can trigger that kind of response.

This is not a political issue. It is a human decency issue. I challenge your audience to ask how you might feel if you were one of the scores of people who came home on September 11th to hear a message left on your answering machine. You could hear the panic in your husband's or dad's or mother's voice as they told you for the last time that they loved you, only to have the call suddenly end, leaving you to wonder, 'Did they die right at that moment?'

Almost ten years later, do you think the pain has subsided for those people? Do you not realize that for many, even the act of physically going to that part of Manhattan will forever trigger the most horrific memories anyone could endure? And now the newspapers and the evening news broadcasters are vomiting it all up again—just so that we can show the world that we are tolerant?

The host never interrupted me once. He didn't speak at all until it was time for a commercial break. His voice was somber as he closed, "Well, you've certainly given us something to think about."

I drove to the nearest rest area and sat there listening to the final hour of his show. The first caller after the break was a young guy who sounded like a twenty-something.

"Wow man, that last dude was really a bummer. It comes down to this man—those people in New York just had a lousy Karma."

I put my face in my hands and wept. Right then and there, I resolved that as long as I was alive, I would never let people forget what took place on 9/11. We must not assume that the facts will be passed on to future generations accurately. Over time, memories can be extinguished. Facts can give way to revisionist narratives. As an eyewitness, I have the responsibility to speak up when history is being misrepresented.

So it's important for me to remember these events and to share them with others. As I remember, I often reflect on the history and nature of God's dealings with His creation and His creatures. How can a loving Heavenly Father allow desolations like 9/11 to happen?

What are we to make of it all?

I contend that, though completely horrific, 9/11 was not a stand-alone event. There has been a steady erosion, a relentless attack, on all that our nation once held dear. Some might label me a dinosaur because I believe that America and her founding are inextricably tied to the God of the Bible. What I don't believe is that America is exclusively a Christian nation. I don't believe that the religious freedoms our fathers and grandfathers died to preserve are only for Christians.

On the contrary, the founders intentionally enshrined freedom of religion as a right. I am not enamored with slogans and bumper stickers. I don't shout, "America—Right or Wrong." But I won't be forced to shout, "America—Always Wrong" either.

We are a nation under siege. As we approach the twentieth anniversary of that terrible, sunny September morning in New York City, my prayer is that I can give insight and hope to a nation, and a world, that is under attack by an ancient enemy.

AMERICA'S CURRENT PREDICAMENT

Twenty years since that terrible day, we find ourselves in a major predicament. Rubble is once again accumulating in major cities all across America. Whole neighborhoods are ruined. Tribalism is on the rise. And families are in turmoil. The national unity which took place immediately during the aftermath of 9/11 didn't last very long. Today we are a nation divided. The accumulated debris of our own making is immobilizing and isolating us, as well as threatening the future of our children.

As I write this, the entire world is in the grip of a pandemic. In Oregon, where I live, we have endured unprecedented lockdowns of selected enterprises. Churches have been singled out by the state for draconian isolation measures and hastily drafted, ever-changing scrutiny by the governor.

"You cannot meet in person."

"You may not sing!"

"Communion must be delivered in sealed, sanitized, pre-packaged, officially-approved elements."

And the list goes on.

The governor of California has publicly advocated for lifting your mask off to take a bite of food and then immediately replacing the mask until the next officially sanctioned morsel can pass your lips. Contact tracers have been hired to track down those violating the edicts of the governor. Stunning numbers of small businesses are permanently shutting their doors.

Notable exceptions to these capricious fiats are marijuana dispensaries and Planned Parenthood facilities, which haven't missed a day of business because they are deemed 'essential.' Meanwhile some cancer and cardiology patients are deemed to be 'elective' cases. At the same time, a new term has entered the national conversation—Deaths of Despair.

Schools are in a state of chaos as the rules change almost weekly. Suicides and domestic violence cases are off the charts. In Canada, the premier of the province of Ontario brazenly admitted that his province is listing suicides as pandemic deaths—and the media ignored it.

In perhaps the most egregious overreach of all, elderly patients are dying without their spouses or their children, who are forbidden from being there to hold their hands. A recent video showed how one hospital is demonstrating great improvisational skills by rigging up an apparatus attached to the ICU bed. The little arm holds up an iPad with the camera aimed on the dying person's face—so their loved ones can "be with them" as they breathe their last breath.

Some nursing homes are "allowing" loved ones to view grandma through screens or plexiglass windows. The sight resembles people viewing animals at the zoo.

Never willing to pass up what they see as a good opportunity, globalist politicians are using the pandemic pandemonium to roll out their socialist agendas. One enterprising government official said it is necessary to "put the Constitution on hold." All these breathtaking developments have us on our heels wondering what is coming next. There is a knot in every stomach, angst in the body politic, and great anxiety around the globe.

The prophet Haggai was 70 years old when he prophesied. He had witnessed the destruction of Solomon's temple. His entire ministry took place during a four-month period. Numerous times he used the phrase "Give careful thought to your ways." I for my part have been doing just that. "Your ways" can be taken as singular, as in one's personal ways. It can also be plural, meaning the corporate response of a nation or people to the Word of the Lord.

> Haggai cried out, "This is what the Lord Almighty says: 'In a little while I will once more shake the heavens and the earth, the sea, and the dry land. I will shake all nations, and what is desired by all nations will come, and I will fill this house with glory,' says the Lord Almighty"
>
> — HAGGAI 2:6-7 NIV

In 2021, world leaders are promoting what they call the Great Reset. The motto for the movement to global governance and the abolition of national sovereignty is: *Build Back Better*.

My question is, "How did we build back after 9/11, and are things better?"

A phrase from a sermon I preached years ago seems timely right now, "Past Is Prologue." To answer the questions I just posed—and many other questions facing us right now—I appeal to the past and go back to the morning of September 11th, 2001.

It was a Tuesday, and I was still asleep . . .

2

THE CHIRPS OF GROUND ZERO

"TURN ON YOUR TV."

My friend didn't even bother with a hello. Like millions of Americans, I was awakened that fall morning to a sickening sight. The World Trade Center was on fire. Still not fully alert to what I was seeing, I immediately thought of my niece and nephew, who both worked in Manhattan.

As reporters tried to keep up with the unfolding nightmare, horrific scenes began to appear. People trapped on the top floors frantically waved at the media helicopters, but the people in the helicopters were powerless to attempt any kind of rescue. Near the sight of impact, where windows once encased their offices, people clung to the structural fragments of the building, desperately trying to escape the smoke and heat of the flames. These people were completely exposed and helpless.

My heart broke.

How could this be happening?

And then I witnessed the unimaginable.

Oh my God . . . jumpers! Dear Lord Jesus . . .

Just as it seemed that time was standing still, another plane hit the second tower. This was no accident.

What did the reporter say—the Pentagon too?

Where on earth is Shanksville? Are we at war?

While the media coverage grew to include Shanksville and the Pentagon, a final horror in New York City took place live on the television screen. The South Tower of the World Trade Center collapsed. In less than a minute, the massive 110-floor building was reduced to rubble. The North Tower followed suit just 28 minutes later.

As a Navy Reserve chaplain, I knew my life was about to change. As the pastor of a local church, I knew I was going to have to be present and attentive to the needs of my congregation. But, as a husband and a father, I had all sorts of personal concerns racing through my mind while the day wore on.

Is my seabag packed? Who am I supposed to report to? Will my family be safe? Does Judy know where my will is?

CRITICAL INCIDENT TRAINING

In April of 1995, I was in Maryland attending a conference for training on how to respond to critical incidents and disasters. The International Critical Incident Stress Foundation was in the middle of a series of excellent training sessions when all of a sudden, the conference was cut short. It was announced that the presenters were all being dispatched to Oklahoma City to help at the site of a bombing that had just taken place.

One of the last things I learned at that training in

Maryland was how to conduct a Critical Incident Stress Debriefing—an exercise that I would participate in many times over the years. One of the phases of a debriefing is known as "the fact phase." This is the part where each participant identifies themselves, tells the others why they were at the incident, and describes what their role was:

I'm Bill. I was the first EMT on the scene. I was treating victims.

I'm Tom. I was the incident commander. My job was coordinating all of the different first responders.

I'm Betty. I was the ER Nurse who helped triage the victims at the hospital.

I'm Craig. I was the dispatcher who handled all of the 911 calls.

In the next phase, which is called "the thought phase," the leader goes around the circle again and asks each participant this question: "When you finally had time to process what had happened that day, when you went off of autopilot and had to time to reflect, what was your first thought?"

AN INNER CALLING

It was hard to find sleep on the night of September 11th, 2001. As I lay in bed after a day of non-stop exposure to the unfolding tragedy, my first thought was tied to the last image I saw before turning the television off.

By now the networks all had their assets deployed, covering every possible aspect of the historic day, using every angle afforded them—including aerial shots from helicopters. There was one final clip showing the devastation from above. The smoke. The fires. And the first responders who climbed the precipitous rubble searching for survivors. They had formed a bucket brigade. All of this together made for a surreal scene.

Somehow, in my heart, I knew I would soon be down inside of that chasm in Manhattan, helping those people in the bucket brigade.

The news anchor had the sense to be quiet and let the film speak for itself. You could hear sounds you might hear at construction sites. But almost like white noise in the background, there was another sound. I recognized it as being familiar, but I couldn't identify it.

What is that eerie sound?

Pretty quickly, it became apparent that search-and-rescue was an extremely dangerous undertaking.

In what would become known as one of the largest crime scenes in American history, Ground Zero was a massive pile of rubble with sharp pieces of steel amid huge fires and immeasurable amounts of ash. The pile of rubble was completely unstable. Rescue workers faced constant danger as they tried to maneuver around what was left of these massive buildings. Many of them wrote their names somewhere on their body in case they got trapped in the rubble.[1]

After enough time passed, construction crews began using heavy equipment to help by removing unstable material, building temporary roads, and hauling away debris. However, the work remained dangerous. The editors of History.com noted, "Every time a crane moved a large chunk of debris, the sudden rush of oxygen intensified the flames. Downtown Manhattan reeked of smoke and burning rubber, plastic, and steel."[2]

In spite of the immense danger, the bucket brigade was the

only option for trying to rescue people early on. For that reason, many brave rescue workers faced the dangers head on and did whatever they could to possibly bring someone—anyone—out alive.

THE SOUND

I couldn't take my eyes off the screen as the news coverage opened a 24-hour window into everything that took place at Ground Zero. And there was that eerie sound that continued throughout the coverage.

What is it?

It reminds me of something, yet I can't quite place it.

It sounded like the smoke alarm in your house when there is a power outage. It also sounded a lot like crickets on a sultry summer night. Commentators on that early aerial footage at Ground Zero called it "chirping." As it turned out, what I saw that first night on TV and—more to the point—what I heard, was the sound of firefighters buried in the rubble.

Firefighters wear a Personal Alert Safety System (PASS) device that sounds an alarm to notify others when they are in trouble. If the firefighter in question still has the ability, they can trigger it themselves. But the alarm can also be triggered automatically when a firefighter has not moved for a certain amount of time.

That haunting sound from the pile as I watched news coverage was the chirping of PASS alarms from 300 heroic souls who were trapped.

They are alone . . .

They are unable to move . . .

Their supply of oxygen is running out . . .

Twenty years after the 9/11 attacks, there is another type of rubble and a whole lot of noise taking place in our nation. But still, if you listen carefully, there are other sounds. Warning sounds. Distress calls.

We ignore the chirps at our peril.

It is far too easy to become accustomed to reports of terror attacks and natural disasters. We cannot allow ourselves to be accustomed to rubble or reconciled with ruin. There are clear warning signs in history of impending disaster. And there are most certainly prophetic warnings in the Bible.

THE VOICE OF JEREMIAH CALLS OUT TODAY

Jeremiah the prophet has been called the weeping prophet. In the book of Lamentations, he describes himself as "the man who has seen affliction." His name has entered our modern lexicon as being associated with "a literary work or speech expressing a bitter lament or a righteous prophecy of doom."[3] We refer to such an utterance as a "Jeremiad."

In the confinement of the palace courtyard prison, Jeremiah heard the Word of the Lord. As he languished in prison, he could hear the battering rams of the Babylonians besieging the walls of Jerusalem. He was uncertain about his fate. Would he soon be executed? Would he be killed during the siege? His crime was that he dared to speak truth to power. He gave the Word of the Lord to the king in Jerusalem and the king didn't like the message. King Zedekiah chose instead to attack the messenger.

While Jeremiah was still confined in the courtyard of the guard, the word of the Lord came to him a second time: "This is what the Lord says, he who made the earth, the Lord who formed it and established it—the Lord is his name: 'Call to me and I will answer you and tell you great and unsearchable things you do not know.' For this is what the Lord, the God of Israel, says about the houses in this city and the royal palaces of Judah that have been torn down to be used against the siege ramps and the sword in the fight with the Babylonians: 'They will be filled with the dead bodies of the people I will slay in my anger and wrath. I will hide my face from this city because of all its wickedness.

— JEREMIAH 33:1-5 NIV

CALL TO ME

It sounds so simple. Yet it is often the very last thing that we do in a crisis. We fret. We panic and we despair. But immediately going to prayer? Not so much. Pastor Jack Hayford once told the story of a lady who came to see him in a counseling session. The lady was in great distress. "Pastor we've tried everything. Nothing is working. I guess all we can do now is pray." Jack smiled and lovingly asked, "Has it come to that?"

Many Bible commentators agree that over a hundred years before it happened, Isaiah prophesied about the exact situation Jeremiah faced in Jerusalem:

Your choicest valleys are full of chariots,

and horsemen are posted at the city gates.
The Lord stripped away the defenses of Judah,
and you looked in that day
to the weapons in the Palace of the Forest.
You saw that the walls of the City of David
were broken through in many places;
you stored up water
in the Lower Pool.
You counted the buildings in Jerusalem
and tore down houses to strengthen the wall.
You built a reservoir between the two walls
for the water of the Old Pool,
but you did not look to the One who made it,
or have regard for the One who planned it long ago.
The Lord, the Lord Almighty,
called you on that day
to weep and to wail,
to tear out your hair and put on sackcloth.
But see, there is joy and revelry,
slaughtering of cattle and killing of sheep,
eating of meat and drinking of wine!
"Let us eat and drink," you say,
"for tomorrow we die!"

— ISAIAH 22:7-13 NIV

Isaiah 30 is another passage relevant to what the Israelites would experience at the hands of the Babylonians. My NIV study bible introduces Isaiah chapter 30 with this heading: "Woe to the Obstinate Nation."

In this chapter of the book of Isaiah, we read:

This is what the Sovereign LORD, the Holy One of Israel, says:
> "In repentance and rest is your salvation,
>> in quietness and trust is your strength,
>> but you would have none of it.
> You said, 'No, we will flee on horses.'
>> Therefore you will flee!
> You said, 'We will ride off on swift horses.'
>> Therefore your pursuers will be swift!
> A thousand will flee
>> at the threat of one;
> at the threat of five
>> you will all flee away,
> till you are left
>> like a flagstaff on a mountaintop,
>> like a banner on a hill."
> Yet the LORD longs to be gracious to you;
>> therefore he will rise up to show you compassion.
> For the LORD is a God of justice.
>> Blessed are all who wait for him!

People of Zion, who live in Jerusalem, you will weep no more. **How gracious he will be when you cry for help**! As soon as he hears, he will answer you. Although the Lord gives you the bread of adversity and the water of affliction, your teachers will be hidden no more; with your own eyes you will see them. Whether you turn to the right or to the left, your ears will hear a voice behind you, saying, "This is the way; walk in it."

— ISAIAH 30:15-21 NIV

Even though it is often our SOS, prayer is not supposed to be simply "our last resort." God wants us to stay in constant communication with Him. Repeatedly, God tells us to "call out to Him." When Jesus taught his disciples to pray, He said, "When you pray, say . . ."

There is something powerful about praying out loud. When we pray out loud it's as if our words have entered history. Calling out to God audibly is an affirmation that we know there is a God who hears us!

When we hear that someone is facing a crisis, we automatically respond "I will pray." We all do it. In our modern context, such as a Facebook post or an Instagram message, we may hit the *Like* button or maybe even add a praying hands emoticon. Public figures holding press conferences after a disaster often say things like, "Our thoughts and prayers go out . . ."

When we say that, we mean it sincerely. But we rarely stop and pray out loud.

THE CHIRPS FROM THE PILE WERE MEANT TO BE HEARD

Jeremiah, after prophesying to the king again, was thrown into a cistern. He was left to die, up to his neck in mud.

He could not move.

His air supply was being depleted.

He was sure he was going to die.

All he could do was call out to God.

Doesn't that describe all of us in certain trials in our lives?

We are unable to move. We are literally up to our necks in trouble. Over time, each successive failure or disaster has left rubble that accumulates to the point that it immobilizes us. All that is left for us is to cry out to God.

The psalmist wrote:

> Out of the depths I cry to you, LORD;
>> Lord, hear my voice.
> Let your ears be attentive
>> to my cry for mercy.
> If you, LORD, kept a record of sins,
>> Lord, who could stand?
> But with you there is forgiveness,
>> so that we can, with reverence, serve you.
> I wait for the LORD, my whole being waits,
>> and in his word I put my hope.

> — PSALM 130:1-5 NIV

In the book of Lamentations, we read about the horrible conditions during the siege, but we also hear how the Lord answered Jeremiah's plea from the cistern:

> My eyes will flow unceasingly,
>> without relief,
> until the LORD looks down
>> from heaven and sees.
> What I see brings grief to my soul
>> because of all the women of my city . . .

> They tried to end my life in a pit

and threw stones at me;
the waters closed over my head,
and I thought I was about to perish.
I called on your name, LORD,
from the depths of the pit.
You heard my plea: "Do not close your ears
to my cry for relief."
You came near when I called you,
and you said, "Do not fear."
You, Lord, took up my case;
you redeemed my life.

— LAMENTATIONS 3:49-51, 53-58

NIV

It is my strong belief that when Jeremiah was trapped in the mud in that cistern, he could hear the echo of his voice resounding as he called to God to spare his life.

VICTIM 0001

As I heard the chirps those first few days, I began to prepare myself. While contemplating what to do or what to say when I first arrived in New York, I remembered one more gut-wrenching image from the first few days of TV coverage. The very first victim whose body was recovered from the rubble had been tagged as "Victim 0001."

Revered fire department chaplain Father Mychal Judge was the first body delivered to the medical examiner. His death certificate would record that the cause of death was murder. As I found out more about him, I learned that he used to carry a written prayer with him to hand out to the firefighters. His prayer would serve as one loud "chirp from the pile." It would also set the tone for the journey on which I was about to embark—a journey that would change my ministry and the trajectory of my life.

Lord, take me where you want me to go.
Let me meet who you want me to meet.
Tell me what you want me to say,
And keep me out of your way.

— FR. MYCHAL JUDGE

In the weeks to come, I would learn that thousands of people from all over America heard the chirps and would find their way to a place called "the Pile."

A DARKNESS THAT COULD BE FELT

Indeed, the darkness shall not hide from You,
But the night shines as the day;
The darkness and the light are both
  alike to You.

— PSALM 139:12 NKJV

I VIVIDLY REMEMBER the first time I heard someone refer to Ground Zero as "the Pile." It bothered me. Like most people, the first I saw of Ground Zero was by watching the 24-hour news coverage of those first few days.

During an interview segment with a New York firefighter, he referred to the place where he did his Ground Zero rescue work as "the Pile."

Surely they could call it something else.

"The Pile" sounded so stark, so final, so crass. After all, thousands of people were buried in it.

How could we all be so disrespectful?

Whenever I heard the word 'pile' I thought of garbage, refuse, waste.

Ground Zero, NYC, September 17th, 2001 U.S. Navy photo by Chief Photographer's Mate Eric J. Tilford

This was not a pile. It was, at least for those first few nights, a place where every American held out hope of finding people alive. Maybe trapped. Maybe injured. But alive in those air pockets beneath the smoking ruins of what used to be the Twin Towers. That's what everyone was still hoping for.

I remember the rescue dogs who braved the jagged debris and the spongy, unstable ground to find signs of life. They walked steadily on unstable ground which was soaked in jet fuel and aerosolized carcinogens. These four-footed heroes were burning the pads of their paws as they climbed a mountain made of pulverized concrete, shards of glass, and rebar which stuck out like bamboo spikes placed in a booby trap.

And no one can forget seeing the firefighters, policemen, and rescue workers searching for the fallen.

Inspired by their bravery, I contacted the Office of the Chief of Chaplains the next day, volunteering to do anything I could to help. Within a week or so, I had orders to report to Manhattan.

THE FIRST WORLD TRADE CENTER ATTACK

Mention "the World Trade Center attack" and most would probably assume you meant the event that took place on September 11th, 2001. However, there was a bombing at the World Trade Center in 1993, even though many may have forgotten about it.

The terrorists used a truck bomb, which was detonated below the North Tower. A group of Islamic radicals were quickly identified as being responsible, and most were arrested within a short time. However, the main organizer of the attacks, Ramzi Yousef, escaped for a time to Pakistan before eventually being brought to justice.

When Yousef was arrested, he admitted everything to a federal agent, explaining that their intent had been for the North Tower to topple over into the South Tower. Their plan was to bring both towers down completely, and they had hoped to kill as many as 250,000 people.[1]

Let the gravity of that sink in.

Fortunately, the terrorists were not nearly as successful as they had hoped. But they did murder six people, including a pregnant woman. They injured another thousand. And somewhere around 50,000 people were evacuated that day, so their hope for such a high number of murders was not completely unrealistic.

According to official government documents and news reports, the attack was planned by a terrorist cell that included Ramzi Yousef, Mahmud Abouhalima, Mohammad Salameh, Nidal Ayyad, Abdul Rahman Yasin, and Ahmed Ajaj. Further reports indicate that they received financing from Khalid Sheikh Mohammed, Yousef's uncle.

In March of 1994, four men were convicted of carrying out the bombing: Abouhalima, Ajaj, Ayyad, and Salameh. The charges included conspiracy, explosive destruction of property, and interstate transportation of explosives. In November of 1997, two more were convicted: Ramzi Yousef, the organizer behind the bombings, and Eyad Ismoil, who drove the truck carrying the bomb. Yousef was also convicted of conspiring to kill Americans by blowing up airplanes.

A document was recovered from Ayyad's office during the investigation. The conspirators had drafted a letter which they intended to send to the press. In that letter, they expressed disappointment over the effectiveness of their attack. They noted that their "calculations were not very accurate this time" but indicated that they would continue to target the WTC, and warned that their calculations would be more precise in the future.[2]

Their stated intent—and the planning and patient

preparation they displayed in carrying out their attacks—coupled with the precision of the 9/11 attacks in 2001, bear the earmarks of a siege. Clearly, the U.S. was put into a defensive position, so much so that a state of the art anti-terrorism response center was constructed after the 1993 bombing. This response center was to serve as the Command Post for Emergency Services in the event of another attack. However, it was strategically located in the worst possible place: The World Trade Center!

When the planes hit the Twin Towers, the Response Center was destroyed, so the initial response to the 2001 attack was coordinated and headquartered in an armory in Manhattan. There were hardly enough phone lines, let alone sophisticated communication networks to begin addressing the crisis properly during those early hours and days. Yet, within twelve days, leaders had performed a minor miracle and set up an efficient Command and Control Center that was functioning effectively.

THE DARKNESS OF GROUND ZERO

When I finally arrived in New York, it was late at night. I rented a car and drove to Battery Park, not far from Ground Zero. I had to go through numerous check points and had my ID and orders scrutinized more than once. Armed guards ran a mirror under my rental car looking for explosives. I remember thinking, 'It *feels* dark.'

I had felt this way on another dark day in American history. I was twelve years old when the nuns hustled us from our school room into the cathedral to pray. It was the afternoon of Nov. 22nd, 1963. President Kennedy had been shot. I remember feeling strange. Although the cathedral was well lit, I *felt* a darkness.

Time Magazine writer Lance Morrow described that day well when he said, "The real 1960s began on the afternoon of November 22, 1963 . . . [It] came to seem that Kennedy's murder opened some malign trap door in American culture, and the wild bats flapped out."[3]

As I looked around Battery Park and saw the anxious looks on the faces of the guardsmen in their combat gear, and the massive number of law enforcement vehicles filling the streets, I thought of the phrase "darkness that can be felt."

In the book of Exodus, God sent plagues upon Egypt to convince Pharaoh to let His people go. He had already turned the Nile to blood. He had sent frogs, gnats, flies, and a plague upon the livestock. Then the Egyptians were afflicted with boils, hail, and locusts. Just before the final blow—the death of the firstborn—God told Moses "Stretch out your hand toward the sky so that darkness spreads over Egypt —**darkness that can be felt**" (Exodus 10:21 NIV).

Against the backdrop of a darkness that could be felt, I finally got to where our team of chaplains was assembled. The next morning, we traveled across the bridge to Ground Zero. When I finally walked up to where the Twin Towers once stood, I could not get my head around what I was seeing.

I remember the footage of Berlin after the Allies bombed it. I also saw newsreel shots of Hiroshima and Nagasaki, but *me* standing there, looking at that yawning chasm of destruction? There are no words adequate to express how small I felt, and how immense the debris field was. At that

FROM RUBBLE TO REDEMPTION

moment I concluded that *'the Pile'* was exactly the right phrase after all.

In the Bible, Nehemiah also had to view "the pile" that was present in his day. Mountains of debris and destruction were the only things left after multiple sieges by the Babylonians. Nehemiah attempts to describe what he saw when Jerusalem was reduced to a tragic pile.

> So I came to Jerusalem and was there three days. Then I arose in the night, I and a few men with me; I told no one what my God had put in my heart to do at Jerusalem, nor was there any animal with me, except the one on which I rode. And I went out by night through the Valley Gate to the Serpent Well and the Refuse Gate, and viewed the walls of Jerusalem which were broken down and its gates which were burned with fire. Then I went on to the Fountain Gate and to the King's Pool, but there was no room for the animal under me to pass. So I went up in the night by the valley, and viewed the wall; then I turned back and entered by the Valley Gate, and so returned . . . Then I said to them, "You see the distress that we are in, how Jerusalem lies waste, and its gates are burned with fire."
>
> — NEHEMIAH 2:11-15, 17 NKJV

Nehemiah does not seem to be able to come up with any eloquent or descriptive words, and I think I understand how he felt.

47

MY FIRST DAY WORKING THE PILE

It is customary in the Navy for the person leaving an assignment to give a 'turnover' file or tour to his or her replacement. In this instance, the person giving us the turnover at Ground Zero walked us through the site; pointing out where the towers were, and how many buildings on the perimeter were dangerously damaged.

I remember looking far off in the distance and seeing an I-beam protruding from the top story of a neighboring building. It stuck out like a giant toothpick. Noticing that I was staring at it, a guy in a hard hat came over to me. I commented, "That must have happened when one of the planes clipped it."

"No, chaplain," the man replied. "That beam didn't come from that building."

I would later learn that the explosion was so violent and the force of the blast so strong, that it was entirely possible for a beam from one of the towers to fly like a javelin and strike this building, which was almost a block away. Human remains were also found on the roofs of neighboring buildings for months and even years after 9/11.[4]

In the middle of our turnover, the chaplain had us huddle around so he could give some vital instructions. "Listen up! This is very important! If you hear one long blast from the horn, stop whatever you're doing. Shut up. And don't move. It means they may have heard something or found someone. If you hear two blasts, run! That means one of these damaged buildings is about to go or part of the Pile is collapsing."

Sadly, I heard the one long blast on many occasions during my time at Ground Zero, only to see groups of rescuers carry a basket up the Pile and then later return with a flag-draped body . . . or part of a body. The respect and honor given to each victim became a ceremony that united all of us at the Pile.

Everyone stopped . . .

Lines formed . . .

Everyone saluted . . .

The ambulance backed in and slowly drove off . . .

And work at the Pile continued.

THE REALITY OF DEATH

At one point on that first day at Ground Zero, just before our exit, I saw a firefighter resting on his pack near one of the vehicles. I approached him from the side. In one of the few pictures I have of me talking to people at the site, neither of us is looking at the other—we are both staring at the Pile.

The only thing I could say was, "It's hard to get your head around it." I said that phrase dozens of times in the next two weeks. It seemed the only respectful way to approach someone who had been working the Pile. I learned that this man had lost many firefighters from his firehouse. In fact, he had been sleeping by his truck. This anguished but determined firefighter had not been home in twelve days. And this was only the beginning of his work at the Pile.

As we left the Pile that first day, I experienced another practice that drove home the reality of death which surrounded all of us at Ground Zero. Before we were cleared to leave the site, two men in yellow HAZMAT suits came up to me and washed my boots. The concern was that the toxic material had to be contained and not disseminated throughout the city.

This was the first time I became acutely aware of the very real possibility that there might be human remains on my boots. It was also the first time that I got completely still. I stood there as my boots were being cleaned and stared at the Pile through moist eyes.

Lord from a darkness we can feel, and from the depths we cry out to you, "Oh Lord, hear our prayer."

4

SOUND THE STILL

IT WAS hard to process the fact that human remains could be so microscopic that they indeed might be on my clothing, my shoes, and even my hands if I touched what would become the "hallowed ground" of the Pile. As I was being 'decontaminated' at the end of my first day, I thought about the training I had that morning. The reminder reverberated in my mind—if we heard "one long blast at the Pile" we were to stop, be quiet, and do nothing but stand completely still. I thought of the famous words every Christian remembers from Psalm 46.

"Be still and know that I am God."

After my team was cleared to leave Ground Zero that night, we had a debriefing. Then I went back to my room and read the entire Psalm. It begins:

God is our refuge and strength,
A very present help in trouble.
Therefore we will not fear,

Even though the earth be removed,
And though the mountains be carried into
the midst of the sea;
Though its waters roar and be troubled,
Though the mountains shake with its swelling.

— PSALM 46:1-3 NKJV

The Psalmist concludes with these stunning words:

Come, behold the works of the LORD,
Who has made desolations in the earth.
He makes wars cease to the end of the earth;
He breaks the bow and cuts the spear in two;
He burns the chariot in the fire.
Be still, and know that I am God;
I will be exalted among the nations,
I will be exalted in the earth!
The LORD of hosts is with us;
The God of Jacob is our refuge.

— PSALM 46:8-11 NKJV

After trying to process what I had seen that first day, I felt led to jot down what Psalm 46 *doesn't say*. For example, it doesn't say:
Be still and in your own strength figure out what to do.
Be still and cull through your contact list so you can call an expert on disaster management.
Be still and surf the net for a do-it-yourself webinar.
What the Lord did want me to do in such a devastating

moment—having my boots cleaned while staring at the biggest crime scene in American history—was to "be still" and "know." What was I to know? The same thing we all need to know . . .

KNOW THAT I AM GOD

Tucked into the Psalm where we read "Be still and know that I am God" is the curious phrase, "Come, behold the works of the Lord, who has made desolations in the earth."

The word 'desolation' comes from the late 14th-century word, *desolacioun,* which means "sorrow, grief, personal affliction—the action of laying waste, destruction, or expulsion of inhabitants, and by extension to leave alone, to desert—from de (completely) and solare (make lonely)." To be still is a solitary affair.

Just you, by yourself, contemplating what God is doing. It is during this quiet time with God that our eyes are opened, our hearts are softened, and the Spirit reveals God's wisdom and revelation to us.

In those still moments, I began for the first time to try and get my head around the reality of what I was seeing. Comprehending the revelation that this destruction and desolation had something to do with the God of the Bible.

How can the horrific scene at Ground Zero have anything to do with God?

Be still and know that I am God—I reflected more on the meaning of that instruction, and the specific words God uses. The words "I AM" hearken back to something God told Moses. In Exodus, we read that Moses was worried the people wouldn't believe that God had spoken to him and given him authority to confront Pharaoh. How lonely Moses must have felt as he faced the task of convincing people he had heard from God.

"What should I tell them your name is?"

"Tell them 'I AM' sent you."

Moses had bemoaned the fact that he was inadequate for the task, but the task was given to him anyway. Whatever else was running through my mind that first night, one thought stood out. I felt inadequate to face the enormity of the task before me in New York. "Who am I that I should go to Pharaoh?" asked Moses. God answered, "I will surely be with you."

At the end of day one, I learned my first lesson. This was not about me and my abilities. It was about the Great I AM. My part? Be still and recognize that.

STANDING STILL WHEN CONFRONTED WITH A CRISIS

Years later, as I prepared to speak on one of the anniversary remembrance ceremonies commemorating 9/11, I came across an amazing illustration. In the history of English ships, there was something known as a Boatswain Call. The Call was a musical pipe one could use to play certain notes or combinations of notes. It was worn by officers who would play different notes that would serve as orders to everyone on the ship. Basically, it was an efficient way to give immediate orders to a ship full of men in the old days.

One call played on the pipe was known as the "Still." The Still was a call for everyone to stop what they were doing, remaining completely silent and still. It was often used to call everyone into reverent silence in order to show respect. For example, the Still was used when a junior ship was saluting a more senior ship. Or it may mark someone's retirement, or a funeral service.

But many years ago, it purportedly had another use. When a sudden disaster occurred, such as an explosion or a fire, the Still would be sounded. The purpose was to have everyone stop what they were doing long enough to gather themselves. This was a brief moment for everyone to stop long enough to make a rational assessment of the situation before springing into action.

As I researched the call known as the Still, I thought back to my time serving alongside Marines. When the battalion or company is about to be addressed by the Commanding Officer, everyone is getting into formation, or being "formed up." They are finding their place in ranks.

Once formed up, the first sergeant or the gunny calls out in a loud voice "Stand by!" That is followed with the command, "Company! Attention!"

To be still is not to idly loll about with one's hands in one's pockets. It is to walk always in the awareness that we serve our Lord and must "stand by." We must be ready and attentive to His Word.

The prophet Habakkuk wrote, "I will stand my watch and set myself on the rampart and watch to see what He will say to me, and what I shall answer when I am corrected" (Habakkuk 2:1 NKJV).

Being assigned at the Pile, I understood that I now had the watch and it would be wise for me to adopt an attitude of standing by and being still. There are biblical precedents for the wisdom of standing still when confronted with a crisis.

Moses told the people at the Red Sea, "Stand still and see the salvation of God."

When King Jehoshaphat was hopelessly surrounded and facing impending doom, God told him to command the people to "Set yourselves. Stand ye still."

In these dire situations, God came through.

God parted the Red Sea and destroyed the entire Egyptian army. And the enemy army surrounding Jehoshaphat was destroyed while the people did nothing but praise God.

STANDING STILL IS NOT EASY

One of the most tragic figures in the Bible is King Saul. Saul was anointed by God to be king. He knew that God had supernaturally chosen and helped him. At the beginning of his reign, Samuel took him aside to reveal the plans God had for him. He said, "Stand thou still a while, that I may shew thee the word of God" (1 Samuel 9:27 KJV).

Saul had the problem you and I have—a bias for action. We want to do what seems best to us—something to bring about the outcome we think is fair. When God told Saul to destroy the Amalekites, He made it clear what He wanted to happen: "Now go and attack Amalek and utterly destroy all that they have and do not spare them; but kill both man and woman, infant and nursing child, ox and sheep, camel and donkey" (1 Samuel 15:3 NKJV).

Perhaps Saul thought that was too harsh. Maybe Saul even felt like he had a better idea of how the nation could benefit. Yet, the net result of his actions cost him his kingdom and ultimately his life. "But Saul and the people spared Agag and the best of the sheep, and of the oxen, and the fatlings, and the lambs and all that was good, and would not utterly destroy them; but everything that was vile and refuse that they destroyed utterly" (1 Samuel 15:9 KJV).

When Samuel confronted Saul about his disobedience, he began to shift blame and tried to justify his actions. Samuel responded by saying "Be quiet!" or "Still!"

Yes, waiting and trusting is hard, especially in a crisis. But God is God. Why and when He does what He does, how He does it, and who He uses are issues which are ultimately far above our pay grade.

My wife, Judy, is a classically trained musician, a prodigy who reached university level proficiency (according to the Royal Conservatory of Music Standards) before she went to high school. I remembered her showing me this entry from the 1925 devotional book *Streams in the Desert:*

There is no music in a 'rest' but there is the making of music in it.

In our whole life melody, the music is broken off here and there by "rests," and we foolishly think that we have come to the end of the tune. God sends a time of forced leisure, sickness or disappointed plans, or frustrated efforts.

He makes a sudden pause in the choral hymn of our life, and we lament that our voices must be silent—our part missing in the music which ever goes up to the Creator.

How does the musician read the rest?

See him beat the time with unwavering count and catch up to the next note true and steady as if no breaking place had come in between.

Not without design does God write the music of our life.

Be it ours to learn the tune and not be dismayed at the rests.

They're not to be slurred over, not to be omitted, not to destroy the melody, not to change the keynote.

If we sadly say to ourselves that there is no music in a rest, let us at least not forget there is the making of music in it.

— LETTIE COWMAN

As the HAZMAT team permitted me to step off into my watch at the Pile each day, I was mindful to first heed the sounding of 'the Still.'

FRESH KILLS

Will they finish in a day? Can they bring the stones back to life from those heaps of rubble—burned as they are? . . . Meanwhile, the people in Judah said, "The strength of the laborers is giving out, and there is so much rubble that we cannot rebuild the wall."

— NEHEMIAH 4:2, 10 NIV

AT THE VERY SAME Ground Zero access and egress point where I would be decontaminated each day, there was a steady flow of trucks in and out of the Pile—lots and lots of trucks. This 24/7 convoy was moving debris from the Pile to a site on Staten Island. I asked one of the engineers who was supervising the excavation of the Pile, "Where are they taking all this stuff?" His answer took my breath away.

"Fresh Kills."

Recovery workers sift through Ground Zero debris at Fresh Kills
October 16th, 2001. Photo by Andrea Booher, FEMA News

After some follow-up questions, I learned that New York City has Dutch Origins. A Dutch settlement at the southern tip of Manhattan island sprang up in the early 1600s and was known as New Amsterdam. In 1664, England took over New Amsterdam and renamed it New York.

'Kills' comes from the Middle Dutch word 'kille' which means 'riverbed' or "water channel." "Fresh Kills" was the garbage dump for New York City. It had been officially closed in March of 2001 but it was reopened to accommodate the massive amount of debris from the Pile.

The landfill is immense, and has even been referred to as one of the largest man-made structures in the history of the world. It is estimated to hold 150 million tons of solid waste. According to the New York State Museum website, when Fresh Kills was reopened to process and dispose of material from 9/11, "A total of 108,342 trucks and barges transported material to the Fresh Kills facility on Staten Island, where it was thoroughly sifted to help identify human remains, personal effects and physical evidence from the hijacked planes."[1]

THE ENORMITY OF THE TASK

A man named Richard Marx, the FBI's Special Agent in Charge, was tasked with overseeing the effort.

Over the next ten months, Marx supervised investigators as they spent a total of 1.7 million hours at the landfill sifting through 1.8 million tons of material. He also recognized the emotional gravity of his responsibilities and put great emphasis on returning personal belongings to family members. The remains of 188 of the 1,215 World Trade Center victims whose remains have been identified and returned to their families were recovered at the landfill. In all, they recovered 4,257 human remains; approximately 4,000 personal photographs; over $78,000 in U.S. and foreign currency; 54,000 personal items, including wedding rings, driver's licenses and keys; and 1,358 vehicles, including 102 fire trucks and 61 police cars.[2]

— QUOTE FROM THE SERVICE TO
AMERICAN MEDALS PROFILE ON
RICHARD MARX

Marx had a tremendous responsibility. He developed a plan that dictated how every piece of debris—down to pieces as small as one-quarter inch—would be hand-sifted, sorted, identified, and, if possible, returned to victims' families.

Marx worked on site for almost 12 months, and he actually volunteered for the assignment. During his time at Fresh Kills, he frequently wore a sweatshirt with a latin phrase on the front, *Opus Dei*, meaning "God's work."[3]

New York Times reporters Dan Barry and Amy Waldman described Fresh Kills as a place that was cold and smelly, with methane gas bubbling to the surface every time it rained. They lamented the "mind blurring" monotony of dump trucks, backhoes, and fireworks which were set every now and then to scare off turkey vultures.[4]

I never personally visited Fresh Kills. My area of responsibility was comprised of the Pile, The Morgue, and the Family Center. Out of respect, I didn't take photos of much of what I saw while at Ground Zero. In fact, I did not take a camera with me until my last day in New York. This was, after all, years before smart phones were invented and to me, it would have felt unseemly for me to pull out a camera and take pictures while serving as a Chaplain. To take photos at the Morgue was out of the question. To take snapshots of family members would have been obscene.

I do have an album though—of snapshots in my heart. Some are too painful to describe.

It is worth noting that at all the sites involved with recovery, investigation, and caring for the victims' families, many of the workers were tasked with doing things other than their primary careers. In fact, many were volunteers.

The Times article by Barry and Waldman also described a few personal profiles of people who worked at the site, all of which reminded me of various people I met during my time in

New York. They mentioned Scott Grainer, an Interal Affairs detective who drove 55 miles every morning to arrive by 4 am to start his 12 hour shift. They told of Rev. Michael Harmuth, an FBI chaplain, who was standing nearby when investigators found a purse. He recalled wondering whether the woman had dropped the purse while running to safety, or if the purse was the only thing that remained of her.

It's a safe bet that Chaplain Harmuth has never been the same after ministering at Fresh Kills. I can attest to the fact that no seminary class can prepare you for a moment like the one he experienced looking at that purse. What did the dump truck drivers think as they made their sad deliveries? How did it affect them? What about my HAZMAT friends?

RISING TO MEET THE CHALLENGE

One of the few photos I took my last day in New York was of two men from Chicago who washed my boots every day. One asked me, "I live in Chicago. I heard they were going to blow up the Sears Tower. Is that true?"

I did my best to allay his fears. "No, I haven't heard about anything like that." Years later I learned that I had been wrong —there was evidence of a plot to attack the Sears Tower.

Everybody who worked there had experiences that scarred them. But they got up every day, laced up their boots, donned their hard hats, and did what had to be done. And for some like me, part of our job was representing God and rendering dignity and honor to such ignoble tasks as sifting for wedding rings in the grey rubble that was Ground Zero.

Virtually every confirmed bit of human remains discovered at Fresh Kills was transported to the Morgue in

Manhattan—with a police escort. Rituals of honor developed over time. No one can adequately thank the amazing people who did this horrific work with such resolve, diligence, and professionalism.

The latin phrase on the back of Special Agent Marx's Opus Dei sweatshirt best described their service: *Non-Ignora Mali, Miseris Succurrere Disco.*

Translation: "No stranger to evil, I relieve the suffering of others."

6

THAT WHICH CAN BE SHAKEN

The words "once more" indicate the removing of what can
be shaken— that is, created things—so that what cannot be
shaken may remain.

— HEBREWS 12:27 NIV

IN THE BEGINNING, the recovery process for human remains at
the Pile and Fresh Kills was an arduous task. At the Pile, the
work had to be done by hand because of the danger of air
pockets. Any section of the Pile could collapse at any time, so
at first, the process generally involved engineers guessing
where human remains might be found and then having people
dig by hand or with shovels. Sometimes they used other hand
tools such as rope, pry bars, and axes. Gradually the process
evolved to using an excavator or a grappler.

Workers use heavy equipment to remove the wreckage of the World Trade Center on October 10th, 2001. Photo by Michael Rieger, FEMA News.

In news reports, Samantha K. Smith told the story of her dad, who was intimately acquainted with the process. She described him coming home "enraged and exhausted" after long days of searching for human remains. She spoke of the emotional turmoil he experienced at being able to hand over only small, token items to the loved ones of victims.[1]

Besides searching for human remains and personal belongings, those processing material had to be on watch for anything that might be evidence. This was still a crime scene. It was a grueling task. In my mind's eye, I can still see the faces of those dog-tired, emotionally spent workers at the Pile.

SHAKING AND SIFTING

The amount of material removed from Ground Zero was so massive that trucks alone could not handle the load. The process actually required immense barges to be loaded with material and transported down the Hudson River, which runs between Manhattan and New Jersey. The barges would make their way around to Staten Island, where Fresh Kills was located. Once there, the material would be unloaded onto dump trucks and driven up the hill at Fresh Kills for processing.

Up to 17 barges a day transported the material, which was primarily made up of concrete, steel, and other building materials. There is estimated to have been 1.8 million tons of material removed from Ground Zero.

As with any major disaster, processes developed and evolved as more expertise was brought to bear. A few months into the process, technology from the commercial recycling industry was implemented. Large spinning cylinders were used to remove larger debris from smaller pieces. The smaller pieces were placed on a conveyor belt, which ran through teams of recovery workers. Workers could only remain on the conveyor belt line for 45 minutes at a time in order to avoid vertigo, and other problems which would arise from watching a moving conveyor belt so closely.

Debris from Ground Zero is processed on a conveyor belt at Fresh Kills landfill on October 16th, 2001. Photo by Andrea Booher, FEMA News.

It is remarkable how much attention to detail was needed to find human remains and evidence. The FBI Evidence Response team had to catalog and evaluate every item pulled from the rubble, and forensics workers had to evaluate anything that was suspected of being human remains.[2]

Digging, shaking, sifting, and identifying.

WHEN GOD SHAKES THINGS UP

After all these years since 9/11, and after all that has since transpired in America, one thing that stands out to me is a conversation I had with a colleague from seminary. We were discussing eschatology, which is the study of end times, or 'last things.' We took night classes together and one night we went out to a restaurant after class.

While sitting in a booth discussing theological nuances, my friend picked up a container of sweetener packets. He shook it violently and *Sweet and Low* and *Splenda* packets flew in every direction. Then to drive home the point he was trying to make, he showed me the container with a few packets left in the bottom. He then said, "That which can be shaken will be shaken, so that which cannot be shaken will remain."

I recognized that he was quoting Hebrews 12:26-27 from the New Testament. In this passage, the writer to the Hebrews warns:

See that you do not refuse Him who speaks. For if they did not escape who refused Him who spoke on earth, much more *shall we not escape* if we turn away from Him who *speaks* from heaven, whose voice then shook the earth; but now He has promised, saying, "Yet once more I shake not only the earth, but also heaven." Now this, "Yet once more," indicates the removal of those things that are being shaken, as of things that are made, that the things which cannot be shaken may remain.

Therefore, since we are receiving a kingdom which cannot be shaken, let us have grace, by which we may serve God acceptably with reverence and godly fear. For our God *is* a consuming fire.

— HEBREWS 12:25-29 NKJV

When the writer to the Hebrews speaks of shaking heaven and earth, he is probably referring to an ancient prophecy from Haggai, who prophesied during the time of the return to Jerusalem after the Babylonian Exile.

> "For thus says the Lord of hosts: 'Once more (it *is* a little while) I will shake heaven and earth, the sea and dry land; and I will shake all nations, and they shall come to the Desire of All Nations, and I will fill this temple with glory,' says the Lord of hosts."

> — HAGGAI 2:6-7 NKJV

Some study Bibles note that the writer of Hebrews is tying Haggai's prophecy to the second coming of Jesus, and specifically how Jesus will judge humanity at that time. Other study Bibles mention Deuteronomy 28 as a cross reference— God had warned the Israelites way in advance that there would be serious consequences for disobeying His law.

> "They shall besiege you at all your gates until your high and fortified walls, in which you trust, come down throughout all your land; and they shall besiege you at all your gates throughout all your land which the Lord your God has given you."

> — DEUTERONOMY 28:52 NKJV

Why was the Lord going to allow the siege? The entire 28th chapter of Deuteronomy outlines blessings for obedience to God's law and curses for disobedience. Two things occur to me when I meditate on these Scriptures.

First, God knows everything. If a siege is to take place, it does not escape His notice. Second, He allows His people to suffer serious consequences—including sieges.

The Bible has a lot to say about shaking and sifting. On the eve of His crucifixion, at the last supper, Jesus was preparing His disciples. When reading the Gospels, it is easy to see that they couldn't get their heads around what He was clearly explaining was about to happen. Jesus had just predicted that one of them was going to betray Him.

The New King James Version of Luke 22:24 says, "Now there was also a dispute among them as to which of them should be considered the greatest." What an odd thing. We aren't privy to which disciples were engaged in this discussion, but I found it interesting that it is Peter the Lord addresses next.

> And the Lord said, "Simon, Simon! Indeed, Satan has asked for you, that he may sift *you* as wheat. But I have prayed for you, that your faith should not fail; and when you have returned to *Me,* strengthen your brethren."
>
> But he said to Him, "Lord, I am ready to go with You, both to prison and to death."
>
> Then He said, "I tell you, Peter, the rooster shall not crow this day before you will deny three times that you know Me."
>
> — LUKE 22:31-34 NKJV

There is a lot here for us to consider. Three times Jesus called him 'Simon'—his name before the Lord changed it to

71

Peter. After Jesus predicts Simon's failure to grasp what was going to happen, Jesus again calls him Peter. I don't think I am reading too much into the text when I say that Jesus used the name Simon to remind Peter of what it was like before he met Jesus.

I believe that part of the reason Jesus called him Peter when He predicted his failure was that Peter needed to be forewarned. He was going to be the leader of the disciples after Jesus was gone, and that meant he had a big target on him. In fact, Satan was going to demand that Peter be *shaken and sifted*. Word studies of the language here infer that a literal translation of Jesus' words to Peter would read something more like: "Satan has demanded that you be called to trial—and that the trial be like a violent shaking to the core."

It's safe to say that America was experiencing a violent shaking to it's core at that very moment in time.

THE LESSON OF THE MOUNDS

As the excavators and backhoes dug into the Pile, and as the dump trucks delivered the debris to Fresh Kills, I kept thinking of the word 'mounds.' All that shaking and sifting left behind *mounds*. Then I remembered an explanation I heard many years ago of what the siege of an ancient city looked like.

Battering rams, siege engines, and the sheer repetitive attacks would dislodge some stone from the wall. Those on the wall would respond to attacks by pouring out hot oil and throwing boulders down on the attackers. Remember that often sieges took months—even years. The debris at the base of the wall accumulated over time, eventually forming enough of a mound or hill to comprise a ramp.

One Hebrew word translated as 'shaken' carries with it the idea of something tottering or about to fall. What an appropriate description of the Pile. As the excavators dug into the Pile and retrieved a bucket full of debris, the operator would intentionally shake the bucket to loosen any possible remains. Once the maximum shaking was complete, then the debris was transported by dump truck to Fresh Kills.

Shaking.

Sifting.

Sieges.

Mounds.

Ramps.

Satan.

The Second Coming.

What might it all mean? Whatever else the attacks on 9/11 accomplished, perhaps the most unsettling is the fact that an enemy was able to attack us on our own soil.

As the sifting through the debris continued, my next exposure to the stark reality of what they were finding—human remains—was about to get up close and personal.

David said about him

" I saw the Lord always before me.
Because he is at my right hand,
  I will not be shaken.
Therefore my heart is glad and my tongue
    rejoices;
  my body also will rest in hope,

73

because you will not abandon me to the realm
    of the dead,
you will not let your holy one see decay.
You have made known to me the paths of life;
    you will fill me with joy in your presence.'

— ACTS 2:25-28 NIV

Lord, remind us of our mortality and the temporary nature of our time on this earth. We trust that even when the earth itself is shaken, that which cannot be shaken—the promise of eternity with you—is settled and secure. Comfort the helpers. Reveal yourself to those who mourn. Heal our Land. Amen.

7

A LOT WORSE THINGS THAN DYING

Death may be the King of terrors, but Jesus is the King of
Kings.

— D.L. MOODY

AFTER ROUGHLY THREE hours at the Pile each morning, our
team of chaplains would transition to the medical examiner's
building where a morgue was set up. The first time I saw it, I
thought how much it resembled the fleet hospitals designed to
be set up and used in combat zones—basically like the one on
the old TV show *MASH*.

There were lots of people in scrubs and masks. Numerous
tents were manned by City of New York Coroners, volunteer
Disaster Mortuary Operational Response Team (DMORT),
and forensic workers from around the country who came to
help identify remains.

Going to the Morgue was my first experience walking
around town outside of the Pile. It was strange to see stores

and delis open, running their business as usual just around the block from this sequestered area where the terrible job of identifying and cataloging human remains was underway. As we moved out of the Pile that first time, the first thing I remember seeing was a Salvation Army canteen truck set up to offer water, coffee, and snacks. On the opposite corner was another such station, this one manned by the Red Cross, providing the workers with some respite from their grisly task.

There is one more vivid memory I have of that first day at the Morgue. Looking at a bare plywood wall at the end of the block, I thought this must have been a temporary barricade designed to hide a construction site. I noticed what looked like graffiti, but it didn't look like normal graffiti. Curious, I decided to walk down a little further and investigate.

As I came closer and began peering through the cracks, I realized it was a barrier erected to hide a small fleet of refrigerator trucks. This wall, like so many other sites in Manhattan, had already become a memorial of sorts. First responders, morgue workers, and passers-by wrote on it, drew on it, and stapled pictures to it. Some crayon drawings adorned it as well. My eye immediately was drawn to this one quote someone had tucked away on one section of the wall:

"An event has happened upon which it is difficult to speak and impossible to be silent."

— EDMUND BURKE

The contrast between the elegant prose and the stark reality of the reason for this wall was driven home to me as I was viscerally affected by the smell of death. This plywood wall was the only thing separating me from truckloads of body parts. The stench seemed to hang suspended in the air, and I found myself wishing a strong wind would blow it away. Instead, as the days wore on, I realized that the stink of death clung to my clothes and my hair. More than once I felt like I was going to be sick.

EVEN THE STRONG WERE BROKEN

All through college and then later seminary, I worked full-time in hospitals. I had completed one year of an RN program before I sensed God calling me into the ministry, so I was familiar with death. I had seen cadavers. I had ministered at multiple accident sites and even a few crime scenes. But this was different.

It wasn't that this scene involved more gore and shock. Two things made this uniquely difficult. First, it was the sheer scope of the incident. And second was my proximity to all aspects of it.

Each day we would work at the Pile for three hours, then get into a van and spend three hours at the Morgue, then close the day with the family members of the deceased. I was ministering to the loved ones of people whose remains I had just seen being examined at the morgue. The reality of this was overwhelming at times.

One of the first people I met at the Morgue was an amazing woman who worked for the Medical Examiner. She was still sporting the last vestiges of a shiner under one eye and had a bandage on her forehead. I learned that this doctor, along with others, had been at Ground Zero when the second tower collapsed. She had been struck by debris and she had witnessed jumpers.

Another forensic pathologist, Dr. Judy Melinek, and her husband T.J. Mitchell, wrote a book about their experiences in the field. Their book is called *Working Stiff: Two Years, 262 Bodies, and the Making of a Medical Examiner.*

In this compelling book, they detail their experience at Ground Zero. Melinek also spoke to the New York Daily News about some of her experiences. She recalls when the first victim arrived, and explained that prior to 9/11, she had seen people killed by trains and speeding cars, people who had jumped from buildings, and people who had been burned. But she had never seen anything like this before. In this case, she felt like she was basically seeing all of those things at once.[1]

Melinek also recalls other significant moments, like when they were told that a label and number would be assigned for any specimen of human remains larger than a thumb—and then seeing that they were being given more than 100,000 preprinted labels for the task.[2] The sheer logistics involved with running such an operation as the Morgue were staggering.

I remember being in awe of the courage and professionalism displayed by these folks who had families of their own, and who were now tasked to deal with this horror every day. My assignment was to see them as people dealing with their own emotions, all the while understanding that their assignment had the capability to wound their souls.

Melinek has shared how difficult the task was for her emotionally. She recounts breaking down after finding a picture of a deceased firefighter's son. She ran into the parking lot, put her face in her hands, and cried.[3] This type of experience was not uncommon for people working the Morgue.

The cast of characters working at the Morgue changed frequently. Each day new volunteers from around the country showed up wanting to help. I remember one day receiving what I refer to as a 'prompting by the Holy Spirit.' That's when a believer hears a little voice inside letting them know to do something they probably wouldn't think to do on their own.

On that particular day, I saw three or four young women in scrubs near the entrance of the main building. They seemed troubled and confused. I was across the street having a cup of coffee. They sort of huddled up, and then one of them who seemed to be their leader, was giving some sort of instructions. The Holy Spirit prompted me: "Go over there and tell them you saw them. Then say, 'Can I help you with something?'"

I waited until their 'meeting' was over and tapped the leader on the shoulder. "Excuse me, I was across the street and saw you guys . . . and well . . . Is there anything I can help you with?"

She looked at the crosses on my uniform and started to sob. "We're dental forensic workers and we want to help, but we can't get started without the proper ID badges . . . but we've never been to New York before. We're not sure where to start. We're Christians and we just prayed that the Lord would send someone to help us."

I was able to assure them that I knew where they should go and what they needed to secure the proper credentials. After praying together, we all praised God for his goodness. I learned that we were from the same denomination and I recognized the name of the church that sent them out—I even knew their pastor's name!

There were others I saw at the Morgue every day, and some of them helped me tremendously. Unfortunately, I cannot recall their names all these years later. One of them was the man who oversaw the Salvation Army canteen. He and I would visit over a cup of coffee, and I found him to be one of those rare people who gives their complete attention to others. His countenance ministered peace even in the middle of such a stressful environment.

I learned that he had been to many disaster events, and he shared how the Lord used him to care for the workers. I learned a lot from him, and I like to think I ministered to him as well. Thinking back on it, I kept thinking that he reminded me of someone. I couldn't put my finger on it until recently. Then one day it hit me. *Mr. Rogers. That's it! He reminds me of Mr. Rogers.*

COMFORTING A NATION

I grew up just about an hour and a half away from Pittsburgh, Pennsylvania, where an ordained minister named Fred Rogers pioneered an entirely new genre of television broadcasting. *Mr. Rogers' Neighborhood* really did create a sense of community in a tumultuous era. His slow, steady attentiveness to little children; calming their fears, and addressing the things that caused anxiety was ministry in its purest form. He tackled issues like racism and xenophobia, not by angrily denouncing but by teaching and modeling tolerance, acceptance, and respect.

"Won't you be my neighbor?" had a special meaning for me. Two kids in my neighborhood, Frank and Willie, were always kind to me and my family. Frank loved to sing. He had a real gift. His talent eventually landed him a role on *Mister Rogers' Neighborhood*. His character was named Officer Francois Clemens, and he was actually the first African American to have a recurring role on a children's TV show.

Who could forget King Friday, Lady Elaine, and the rest of the cast, not to mention Daniel Tiger, the one who could express the fears of a small child to the safest of listeners—Mr. Rogers himself.

Mr. Rogers had a long history of helping people heal during difficult times. Almost immediately after his show began airing in 1968, he addressed the dismay and anxiety children felt after events like the assassinations of Martin Luther King Jr. and Robert Kennedy.[4] He tackled topics like nuclear war, the Iran hostage crisis, and the explosion of the space shuttle *Challenger*.

He talked about things like divorce and death, all as part of his ministry to help people cope with life's most challenging times. This approach of helping calm people's fears during times of crisis was no accident. Mr. Rogers explained the origins of this unique ministry, "When I was a boy and I would see scary things in the news, my mother would say to me 'Look for the helpers. You will always find people who are helping.' To this day, especially in times of disaster, I remember my mother's words, and I am always comforted by realizing that there are still so many helpers—so many caring people in the world."[5]

Interestingly enough, Mr. Rogers retired right before 9/11 happened, in August of 2001. But he could not stand by and do nothing to help. New York City held a special place in Fred Rogers' heart—he lived there part-time. Although retired, he quickly went to work producing videos to comfort the nation. In one of the final videos, he said, "Thank you for whatever you do— wherever you are—to bring joy and light and hope and faith and pardon and love to your neighbor and yourself."

My Salvation Army friend at the canteen didn't wear a sweater. He didn't change his shoes and sing "It's a beautiful day." However, my Salvation Army friend did, on more than one occasion, calm people's spirits and fortify their ramshackled emotions by listening to them. The gifts he gave to his frequent confidants were his attention, and a surprisingly effective affirmation that they were in this unusually difficult situation together—two neighbors.

A "YES" FACE

In recalling the Morgue—with its sights and sounds and smells—I am reminded of an illustration I once used in a sermon years ago. The story is told of an event that took place in Colonial America near a bridge. There was a man who used to wait near the bridge to beg alms of all who crossed. An entourage was approaching on horseback. The man jumped out and asked for money.

Suddenly he was surrounded by armed guards. "Don't you know who that is? That's Thomas Jefferson!"

The man replied, "I don't know anything about that. When you stand here all day like I do, begging for help, you recognize that some people have 'No' faces and some have 'Yes' faces. That man has a 'Yes' face."

After the first week of visiting the Morgue daily, I began

to develop relationships with some of the coroners and forensic technicians. Our conversations often took place just outside the tents where they were examining body parts. In some cases they were examining specimens of tissue to see if it was human or animal.

I saw things that I can't ever unsee.

In one instance, I recall seeing the team get excited that they had found someone's ring. Another time, I saw a parcel from the refrigerator truck being opened. The label read, "Female - Stairway 2." The constant reality of so much death was taking a toll on me.

Then one of the DMORT guys came up, and quietly but intentionally, he got in between me and what I was staring at. He put his arm on my shoulder and said, *"C'mon, Chaplain. Let's go get a cup of coffee."*

He had a 'Yes' face.

This caring man told me how he had worked at the Oklahoma City bombing, as well as various earthquakes, floods, and hurricanes. He was a mortician who often volunteered his services on DMORT teams to help during major disasters.

DMORTs operate under the Department of Health and Human Services National Disaster Medical System. DMORT teams are composed of funeral directors, medical examiners, coroners, pathologists, forensic anthropologists, medical records technicians and transcribers, finger print specialists, forensic odontologists, dental assistants, x-ray technicians, mental health specialists, computer professionals, administrative support staff, and security and investigative personnel.[6]

Considering all that this one man had seen in his life and

career, I was surprised that he had the most calming effect on people, and a very comforting voice. He wasn't *trying* to be like that. He was truly like that. He was authentically interested in me. He listened to my story and how I came to be there. Then he looked me in the eye and said matter-of-factly, "You know . . . there are a lot worse things than dying."

Coming from him—knowing what he had seen and smelled and touched—his remark broke the spell of doom that had begun to take over my mind. From that day on, I did two things. First, I periodically took breaks and walked away from the Morgue. I would have a snack or walk outside the perimeter to see that life was still going on all around us. This helped me to stay strong enough emotionally to do the work I was called there to do.

The other thing I decided to do was follow his lead. When I was back at the Pile, I began to intentionally stand between those at the Pile and what they were looking at. As I ministered to them, I wanted to at least give their eyes a break.

Toward the end of my time at the Morgue, it fell to me to give a familiarization tour to Captain Leroy Gilbert, Chaplain of the Coast Guard. Almost immediately, I took note of how tired he looked. I showed him the plywood wall then just backed away as he stood there for a while. He was at the Pentagon on the day of the attack and had acted as a first responder on the scene there. Now here he was in New York. I could only imagine what might be running through his mind as he saw the refrigerator trucks. I only hope that for those brief moments, mine was a 'Yes' face for him.

Before I left the Morgue for the last time, I went back to that plywood wall. I decided to add my own note to the symphony of quotes, sayings, encouragements, and laments. It comes from the prophet Jeremiah who endured the siege of Jerusalem. He had seen his relatives from the priestly class murdered. He watched while the temple was destroyed. Perhaps worst of all, he had witnessed a severe famine, and the cannibalism that resulted from it.

> Remembering mine affliction and my misery,
>   the wormwood and the gall.
> My soul hath them still in remembrance, and is
>   humbled in me.
> This I recall to my mind, therefore have I hope.
> It is of the Lord's mercies that we are not
>   consumed, because his compassions
>   fail not.
>
> — LAMENTATIONS 3:19-22 KJV

As I write this, our country is reeling from a pandemic, violence, fraud, and propaganda. Divisions run deep. Cities are engulfed in flames. Vitriolic accusations are hurled from citizen to fellow citizen, neighbor to neighbor. Anger, hatred, rage, and violence seem to reign in many people's hearts. In a time of siege—like the one we find ourselves in now—we would do well to allow the Holy Spirit to get between us and everything we are watching. We need to listen as He gently encourages us.

"Look for the helpers."

. . .

Oh Lord, thank you for the helpers. Thank you for the man from the Salvation Army, and the mortician from DMORT, and the countless forensic workers who faithfully sifted through remains to identify bodies for the families of those who perished so suddenly and violently. Thank you for the dignity and respect they showed. Thank you for their professionalism which was expressed in their training and the execution of such a grisly task. In Jesus' name. Amen.

8

GRIEVING AT THE PIER

GETTING around New York City in late September and early October of 2001 was a challenge. Our team of chaplains was uniquely blessed, however, to have some amazing logistical assets—not the least of whom was a Coast Guard Reservist who had been called to active duty. This individual was also a member of the NYPD in Manhattan. His assistance was invaluable.

As a Navy Chaplain, ministry to the families who lost loved ones was my most important assignment. Before jumping into that more deeply, I'd like to relay a seemingly random event which took place one morning as our team was about to board the van that would take us to the Pile, then the Morgue, then to a giant pier building on the other side of Manhattan. At that pier building, family members who lost loved ones were dealing with gut-wrenching issues alongside those who were there to help.

As I mentioned in the case of the NYPD detective that helped us so much, many reservists from every branch of the armed forces were called up to respond to the attacks of 9/11. Our driver was just such a man. He was a cheerful, squared away young 'Coastie' who was diligent and helpful as he carried out his assignment to get our team where we needed to be.

One morning I got to the van before the others, and he was sitting behind the wheel, so I decided to chat him up a little.

"Good morning. I haven't had a chance to visit with you. Tell me about yourself. What do you do in your civilian career?"

"I'm attending the NYPD Academy sir."

"Wow that's great . . . " Then I had another one of those Holy Spirit promptings. " . . . so, were you in the city on 9/11?"

"Yes sir. I was driving into the city."

"Did you see anything?"

"Oh, yes sir. I saw the second plane hit the tower."

"You saw it? As you were driving?"

I went into Critical Incident debriefing mode.

"So how are you doing? Sleeping okay?"

"Oh, yes sir. I'm fine."

Just then the team began to show up at the van. I heard a plane go overhead and it just somehow occurred to me to ask one more question as I went to my seat.

"Oh, one more question." I looked up at the sky and asked, "How many planes have gone overhead this morning?"

"Thirteen, sir."

He was subconsciously counting every airplane he heard!

Hyper-vigilance is one of the symptoms manifested by someone who has experienced a traumatic event. I made sure to check in on him every day and thankfully he appeared to be doing very well. I'll bet he went on to become a great cop. For such a young man, he showed great poise and maturity.

That morning may well have been the morning of the very first day we traveled to the piers, I can't recall for certain. But that encounter with our driver prepared me to be intentionally aware that everyone I came across had their own story and their own issues—truly everyone in NYC had been traumatized in one way or another. I especially began to pay attention to those wearing uniforms. Just because they were part of the response to the attacks did not mean that they were not profoundly impacted.

Almost every person in uniform I spoke with had either lost someone or knew someone who had lost someone on September 11th. I've never seen so many different uniforms from so many different agencies and departments in one place. I began to take note of ID badges, rank devices, laminated cards on lanyards denoting security clearances, and jackets with logos:

- FBI
- PORT AUTHORITY
- FDNY
- NYPD
- DMORT
- MEDICAL EXAMINERS
- SALVATION ARMY
- RED CROSS

Each one had a unique story to tell regarding how they ended up as a 'soldier' in this vast army of helpers. Being in the company of some of the most remarkable and compassionate people I'd ever met, I remember wishing I had time to talk at length with each one.

Around the same time I was introduced to the pier, I was also sent up the Hudson River to visit the crew of a Coast Guard Cutter which was guarding the nuclear power plant right off of West Point. There were constant reminders that ours was a fluid situation, and that further attacks were a real possibility. In this instance, I noted that Coast Guard boats normally used for rescue missions now had 50-caliber machine guns mounted. They were patrolling the rivers as a security force.

THE STARE

Driving up toward West Point—which is located on the Hudson River—I had a little time to kill before the Launch was to pick me up and take me to the Coast Guard Cutter. I went into a little bakery and ordered a cup of coffee. While in line, I spotted a fireman with an officer's cap. He was seated in the back of the bakery, decked out in his dress uniform. His demeanor was flat. He appeared to be looking out the window, his gloved hands folded, letting his coffee get cold. He had what I call 'the stare.'

I saw 'the stare' often at the Pile and at the Morgue. It's the look of someone who is reliving a horrible memory. The Fire Captain didn't notice as I walked up to him. By now, I felt comfortable just striking up a conversation with anyone I came across. My uniform had the cross on the epaulets, identifying me as a chaplain. The Holy Spirit works through us in such situations, often in ways that seem small. They can be almost imperceivable unless you're sensitive to it.

At that moment, it just 'occurred' to me that he was either coming or going to one of the hundreds of memorial services for fallen firefighters. I don't believe that observation originated from me.

"Did you do a funeral today?" I asked.

"I do all of them," he said with the saddest look on his face.

He was part of—or may have even been the leader of—the honors detail that conducted all the funerals. They did over 300 in a very short time.

I don't remember his name, but I can still see his face.

I prayed with him and every instinct I had as a pastor told me I should stay and sit with him longer. But no such luxury was afforded to me. I had to get to the rendezvous point and take the Launch out to the Cutter where I heard story after story of crew members—where they were and what they experienced on 9/11.

Many of them knew people who had died on 9/11. They were all wondering if the United States was about to declare war, and if so, where they would be deployed. I held a brief service as we looked out at West Point. I was so proud to be in the company of such amazing Americans who were fighting through their own pain. To stand guard. To honor the dead while simultaneously protecting millions of New Yorkers from further attacks.

The next day it was back to the routine, but with a new addition. Our team would now be visiting the Family Assistance Center (which we called "the Family Center" for short) each day. When we finally got to the place where the families were being cared for, my first thought was that this must have been the largest indoor space I had ever seen. It was cavernous.

The Family Center was set up inside of a building at Pier 94. The piers are massive concrete structures that stretch out into the Hudson and are long enough to be used by cruise liners and other large vessels for loading and unloading. Sitting on top of some of these gargantuan concrete piers are hangar-type buildings that are often used for events like conventions, concerts, and conferences.

As we walked in, our guide pointed out each of the different operations that were going on. Translation services. Legal help. Insurance company representatives. Social workers. Financial assistance.

It was hard to take it all in. Here on that first day at the Family Center, the broader impact of loss hit me. There were quiet places set apart, and there was also a constant flow of people. Young and old. Various ethnicities speaking every language imaginable. Each one with his or her own version of 'the stare.'

One distraught lady came up to me.

"A rabbi . . . Can you find me a rabbi?" she implored.

Even though I had just gotten there and had no clue where anything was located, I assured her I would do my best to find her a rabbi right away. She told me that her husband was an employee of Cantor Fitzgerald.

I had heard some bits of information about the terrible losses endured by Cantor Fitzgerald. In many ways, CEO Howard Lutnik became the public face of all the companies headquartered in the Twin Towers. Their operations were heavily concentrated in the World Trade Center. The losses and the chaos, all the unimaginable devastation to the family members of this huge company, gave America an up close and personal glimpse of the nightmare that was 9/11.

Cantor Fitzgerald occupied the 101st to the 105th floors of the World Trade Center. In an instant, 658 of their 960 New York employees were killed. Early on, Howard Lutnik constantly had microphones shoved in his face. He was peppered with questions that inferred his company wasn't doing enough to help the families—all the while suffering his own personal grief.

Reporters continued to press him about not doing enough to help the families. While addressing that issue one time, Lutnik's countenance began to change. He had 'the stare.' Then he just broke down and began to sob. No longer the controlled measured-response, media-savvy executive in damage control mode, he just broke down and wept. "I'm doing all I can," he confessed through his tears.

In a 2016 interview with NPR, Lutnik described the chaos of being there as Tower Two fell. He talked about how it felt being trapped in the cloud of smoke and ash that enveloped him. Then he talked about his brother:

"My brother Gary was 36, and he was in the building. And later that night when I spoke to my sister, she told me that she spoke to my brother. And she had said to him, oh, my God. Thank God you're not there. You know, thank God you're not there. And he said, 'I am here. And I'm going to die. And I just wanted to tell you I love you.' And he said goodbye. He said—you know, my sister got to talk to my brother when he said goodbye. I still get choked up. Sorry."[1]

Lutnik was charged with helping the grieving families of 658 employees—and making major business decisions that affected his remaining employees and their families—all while grieving the loss of his own brother. Everyone had their own story. Lutnik's story is a reminder that calls of judgment or criticism probably were not wise or helpful.

As I went to find a rabbi, I remembered that the woman said something about 'sitting shiva.' I had a vague memory that the term had to do with the mourning customs of the Jews. Years later I would investigate the Jewish customs of mourning. For now, I had to content myself with hurriedly finding a rabbi for this woman who was beside herself with grief.

THE FACES I COULD NOT HELP

En route to finding the rabbi, I walked past someone speaking Russian. They were trying to communicate with another person regarding an embassy issue, but I had no time to stop and get involved in that situation. I had to move on to the next person who had 'the stare.'

Because I literally wore the cross on my shoulders, people would look at me, expecting me to sit with them and somehow comfort them. It happened on the streets. It happened on the Staten Island Ferry. It even happened when I went in to use the restroom.

In the years following 9/11, this was a recurring theme of my nightmares. Eventually, I sought some help for the PTSD. Even though I have gotten help with it, I still have had this recurring dream for years that involves crowds of traumatized people coming up to me expecting me to be able to help them somehow. The nightmare part is not that they need help—it's that I feel inadequate for the task.

The part that damaged me so much was the sheer

magnitude and scope of the aftermath. The victims' families were so numerous that I was not able to stop and give the care that I would instinctively want to give to every individual who was suffering.

I still see their faces.

I still see the stare.

In the pier building, there were places for the responders to get a hot meal, put their feet up, and try to take a break. On the tables where we ate, there were cards. Hundreds of cards like a tablecloth mosaic, made up of crayon drawings by NYC school kids. Their teachers had them write cards to comfort the families and the first responders.

I was able to bring one back to Oregon with me. It was a crude crayon drawing of a building broken in half, bright red in the middle to show the fire. There was a helicopter with a stick figure looking out on the falling tower. The stick figure was crying. In large letters, the child wrote: DEAR FIREMANS. I AM BOKIN HEATED. THAT IS ALL.

It felt to me like every telephone pole, every space in New York where it was possible to tack on or staple a picture, there were photos of those lost in the Twin Towers. Family members carried photos with them. I had people come up to me on the street. They would see the cross, the hard hat, and the boots, and ask, "Are you down there?" Then they would pull out a photo—often a black and white Xerox copy—of their brother or mother or niece or son or daughter.

This is my daughter. Please, if you find out anything . . .

It wasn't until much later that I began to get some sense of how profoundly this all affected me. Years later, back at my church in Oregon, I was in my office between the two Sunday services. On my way to the sanctuary for the second service, I always made it a point to peek into every Sunday school classroom and love on the kids. This was one of my favorite things to do. I would go up to the five-year-old, resplendent in her princess dress, accessorized with a plastic tiara and sporting rubber boots. I would give her a big hug and tell her how beautiful she looked.

I would listen to the 8-year-old 'mighty hunter' tell me about his exploits with his dad, and how they 'got their elk' that week. I would make note of the little one off to the side who doesn't make much eye contact, as her parents struggled through a nasty divorce.

But this Sunday, another one of my princesses ran toward me down the hallway and yelled, "Pastor Jim, Pastor Jim! Look!"

She was holding her Sunday school paper that she had colored.

Suddenly, I got very dizzy. I felt like I was going to vomit. I started smelling dead people. Turning, I literally ran away from her, back to my office. I locked the door and curled up on my couch.

As I recall that event today, I don't remember how I got through the second service. I do remember the look on my associate pastor's face when he came to get me.

I ended that day at the VA hospital with chest pains. It took me a while to realize what had happened. The little girl trying to show me her crayon-drawn picture triggered a response that took me back to New York. Instinctively, I felt like she was about to ask me for help finding her dead relative.

THE FAMILY CENTER

As I mentioned, it was the sheer scope of the disaster that came into clear focus as I watched what went on at the Family Center. Take the woman from Cantor Fitzgerald for instance. By the time we crossed paths, she had to have assumed that her husband was dead. I couldn't gauge how old she was, but I felt it was safe to assume that she may have had school-aged children.

She had been suddenly cast into widowhood.

In a normal world, she would find the rabbi and observe the mourning rituals. She would have legal issues to deal with. There would be financial issues like pension and insurance. But the one thing that gives people some sense of closure from that initial process was missing. There would be no burial for this widow. There was no body to bury.

What did she tell her kids? What were the kids going through? Though no one was fully aware of it yet, there would be enormous psychological and physical issues. What were the teachers telling their students? What was the city going to do? Would insurance payouts be delayed, or maybe even contested? What would the cause of death be listed as? Murder? Who would watch the kids while this traumatized woman faced all these questions?

I was about to find out the answer to that last question.

The indoor space of the giant pier building was cordoned off—much like the kiosks and curtained-off areas of a trade show. One such area was being used as a giant nursery for little children. When I saw it, one of the first thoughts that crossed my mind was the memory of when the Murrow building was blown up in Oklahoma City. There was a nursery and daycare that had been destroyed in the blast. Firefighters, cops, and EMTs had to carry out the little bodies. In Manhattan, these little ones were victims of another kind— they would grow up without a parent or a sibling or an uncle or a grandparent.

As I watched the little children, two things happened, taking place almost simultaneously. Someone's pet therapy dog went up and licked the face of a little girl. I'm not sure why, but at that exact same moment, a fury began to build in my heart. I distinctly remember the thought that came to mind as if it were yesterday.

An enemy has done this.

Immediately, I tried to push down my indignation and contain my rage.

No time to think about that now . . .

This is only the first hour of my first day at the Family Center . . .

GOD'S COMFORT

And our hope for you is firm, because we know that just as you share in our sufferings, so also you share in our comfort.

— 2 CORINTHIANS 1:7 NIV

PERHAPS YOU'VE BEEN THERE. TSA agents pat you down. You find your gate. The preboarding call goes out. Then they call your section. You cram your carry-on into an overhead bin. The flight attendant reminds you how your seat belt works, and where the exits are. Then he or she pulls out the mask and explains what will happen in the unlikely event of a sudden loss of cabin pressure. The attendant then ends with instructions on how to inflate your life preserver in the event of a water landing.

Two things come to mind when I think about those briefings. First, the majority of people pay no attention at all. Second, in describing the oxygen mask protocol, special attention is given to remind parents to put their own mask on first before putting it on small children. The ones ignoring the briefing probably think, "I have heard all this before, no need to pay attention."

It is helpful to remember that in the cockpit there are other people meticulously going through checklists and protocols, reciting them out loud every time. They have logged thousands of hours in the air and yet they read aloud a pre-takeoff checklist. Every. Single. Time.

When I hear the instructions about putting one's own oxygen mask on first, I am always struck by the fact that the passenger needs to "pull down" the mask to start "the flow." That phrase always reminds me of the need to pray when a crisis arises. When a crisis hits, you must first secure your own supply of inspiration, or you will not be able to help anyone else.

At the midpoint of my time at the Pile, I was about to experience the reality of this important truth firsthand.

THE COMFORTER

To say I was functioning at a high level of adrenaline arousal would be the understatement of the century. The situation was fluid and there were unique challenges almost every hour. One constant for me, however, was this nagging sense that I was not doing enough. My instincts as a local church pastor served me well in some instances while hindering me in other ways. The pastoral ministry principle of simply being present with people who are in pain was very important. But my hardwired desire to want to linger with each person was counterproductive in my role as a chaplain, especially in an incident of this scope.

One day, I hit a wall. I was spent—emotionally and physically. I honestly did not think I could bear to see one more person with 'the stare,' or with tears in their eyes, or clutching a photo of their lost loved one.

Sitting in the back of our van as we traveled to the Family Center, I pulled down my hard hat over my eyes, folded my arms, and assumed a posture meant to signal to the other chaplains that I was napping. But in reality, I was doing something the Bible calls "praying in the Spirit."

The Bible speaks of a kind of prayer that transcends mere words. The Apostle Paul describes it in Romans 8 as "groans that are too deep for words."

For we know that the whole creation has been groaning together in the pains of childbirth until now. And not only the creation, but we ourselves, who have the firstfruits of the Spirit, groan inwardly as we wait eagerly for adoption as sons, the redemption of our bodies. For in this hope we were saved. Now hope that is seen is not hope. For who hopes for what he sees? But if we hope for what we do not see, we wait for it with patience.

Likewise the Spirit helps us in our weakness. For we do not know what to pray for as we ought, but the Spirit himself intercedes for us with groanings too deep for words.

— ROMANS 8:22-26 ESV

After praying that way for a while, I felt refreshed. The

van hit a bump and I sat up, pushed my hard hat back in place, looked out the window, and there it was. A ship had pulled in next to the pier where the Family Center was located. It was there all along, but I had not noticed it before. It was not the usual battleship gray, but rather a dazzling bright white—so bright I had to squint. On her side, the ship's name was written out in huge lettering: COMFORT.

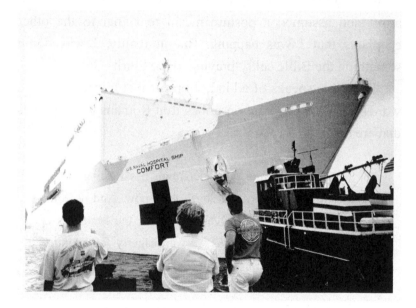

USNS Comfort Photo by United States Department of Defense

In the book of John, Jesus repeatedly refers to the Holy Spirit as the "Comforter." In that moment, looking up at the *USNS Comfort*, I remembered from my seminary days that the Greek word, *parakletos*, which is translated as 'comforter' comes from two other Greek words—*para* meaning "alongside" and *kaleo* meaning "called." So a literal translation might be "called alongside" with the context being one who is called alongside of another to help them.

Some could say that it was a coincidence that the ship just 'happened' to pull alongside and I just 'happened' to set my eyes on her right after my prayer. There was, however, no coincidence about what the Lord spoke to my heart in that moment. It was as if He said to me: "I'm here. I am the Comforter. I will see to it that you will accomplish the purposes I had when I brought you here."

A huge burden lifted from me in that moment. The Holy Spirit was with me, to comfort me during this difficult process. And He had sent many others to come alongside me as well. I was not in this alone. Not even close.

I recalled the advice Mr. Rogers' mother gave him to look for the helpers. There were a myriad of helpers at Ground Zero who dove right in to come alongside others. They gave no thought to how all this sorrow and loss would inevitably affect them. They just came and helped.

"First responders" was a term that would soon be on the lips of every journalist in the world. The term would become synonymous with self-sacrifice, courage, and great love. The hospital ship's mission, I would soon learn, was to give medical attention, respite care, and comfort to the first responders. Someone had to help the helpers, after all.

When I began my public ministry in 1978, a wise pastor gave me some sound advice. He said that a pastor needed three things to survive long term in the ministry:

1. The mind of a scholar
2. The tender heart of a small child
3. And the hide of a rhinoceros

I would, after my experience in New York, add one more thing to his list—the unconditional love and snuffly kisses of a dog.

CANINE COMFORTERS

Around the same time that the *USNS Comfort* arrived, I became more emotionally vulnerable. I had, up until that time, maintained a pretty good game face. I had even developed the ability to compartmentalize things in my mind, so that I could be present and focused. But the sheer nature of the work and the relentless demands of the mission were taking a toll. Seeing the *USNS Comfort* had cracked open my shield a bit— enough for me to start opening up and working through some very strong emotions.

One day at the Family Center, I encountered a lady who didn't speak English. The look on her face captured the devastating effects of 9/11. She kept looking at the crosses on my shoulder boards. Her face was swollen because of her tears. With wild gestures, she did her best to communicate with me. She touched the epaulets of my uniform and began to weep. I prayed for her. As she pulled herself together, I learned that she knew at least one word of English, "Amen." Since we could not communicate any further, all I could do was watch as she disappeared into the mass of widows, widowers, bereaved parents, orphans, and all of the others left to deal with the carnage at the Pile.

Afraid I might break down right there on the spot, I walked to the farthest reaches of the pier building, away from all of the activity. Finding a relatively secluded spot, I sat on the concrete floor, folded my arms into a pillow, and put my

FROM RUBBLE TO REDEMPTION

head on my knees in an attempt to gather myself. I had to be there for others. That meant I needed to prepare for the next encounter. I needed ministry myself, so once again, I prayed in the Spirit.

After a little while, I got the feeling someone was watching me. Then I felt someone breathing on me. I looked up to see a German Shepherd with his head cocked to the side. He seemed to be looking right into my soul. Somehow, I felt released to let the tears flow. And flow they did.

Then the four-footed comforter licked my face. I was so caught up in the moment that I had not yet acknowledged the dog's owner.

"What's his name?"

"Bruno."

After this much needed emotional release and comfort, I thanked the lady, scratched Bruno's ears, and got back to work. I can't describe how important that brief encounter was to me, except to say that soon after, I was able to get back into the fray and help more people.

Bruno was not the first and certainly not the only dog I would see in action at Ground Zero. While the nation's attention was riveted on mayors, governors, and the President, there were other names that were never uttered on the evening news—names like Bruno, Salty, Nikie, Tikvah, Bretaigne, and Riley.

HEROES

There were many animals who helped out in various ways. For example, Nikie was a golden retriever who worked 12 hour shifts at the Morgue. His primary function seems to have

105

been similar to the role Bruno played in my life. He somehow brought comfort. His handler, Frank Shane, founder of the non-profit K-9 Disaster Relief, explains that people felt comfortable unloading their problems to this canine counselor: "There's a special spot, I believe, in everyone that an animal transports you back to as a child. In a disaster setting where your whole world has turned upside down and your trust is wiped out, here comes an animal that psychologically transports you back to a time in life where you felt safe."[1]

Frank also elaborates on the fact that Nikie seemed to carry the emotions home with him. The dog seemed to suffer from nightmares during the first few months, and would often come home, fall down on his bed, and then howl mournfully while asleep.[2]

Omar Rivera was an engineer who worked in Tower One. Being blind, Omar had his service dog, Salty, with him as always. When Omar realized there was an emergency of some kind, he began moving toward the exit with Salty. However, he quickly realized that there was a huge panic and that it was unlikely he would get out alive due to his disability. Thinking quickly, Omar dismissed Salty so that at least he would get out alive. Unwilling to leave his owner behind, Salty came back a few minutes later. After more than an hour of walking down the stairs, Omar and Salty both made it out alive.

Another guide dog, Roselle, led her owner Michael Hingson, to safety right before Tower Two collapsed. After they were safe, they helped lead others to safety, some of whom had been blinded by falling debris.

There was an iconic image of Riley, a canine member of the FEMA Pennsylvania Task Force One, being lifted out of the debris pile at Ground Zero. The bond between human comforters that work in disaster relief and their furry compatriots is very rich.

The notion that dogs have the power to ease human emotional suffering is not new. Anyone who has ever cried in the presence of a canine companion is already fully aware. But most probably don't realize that the history of therapy animals goes all the way back to World War II, when Smoky, a four-pound Yorkshire Terrier went around cheering up wounded soldiers at hospitals in New Guinea.[3]

After working a school shooting in 1998, Cindy Ehlers understood the value of therapy dogs. By 2001, she had trained Tikvah, her Keeshond, for disaster and crisis relief work. According to the American Kennel Club, "Tikva, because of her crisis-relief training, became one of the few dogs who worked at Ground Zero helping the responders. Her preparation for working in this environment, as well as her cute looks, rock-solid temperament, and unusual breed, made her ideal for taking minds off the horror, if just for a few moments."[4]

Some rescue workers reported that therapy dogs were the only thing that helped them make it through the emotionally grueling workdays.[5] God created animals for many purposes, but comfort is certainly one of them. One quote sums up very well how God uses these animals to help human beings.

"Dogs have a way of finding the people who need them, Filling an emptiness we don't even know we have."[6]

— AUTHOR THOM JONES

AN EVER-PRESENT HELP IN MY TROUBLE

The Comforter—the Holy Spirit—is not just a 9/11 first responder. He is not merely a 9-1-1 operator either, although He does respond and dispatch help in every crisis. We must remember that our Comforter is also a companion and guide —a teacher long after the crises in our lives are over—and an ever-present helper, even during our most personal times of need.

The immediate years following my time at the Pile were punctuated with periodic alarming episodes that troubled me deeply. I was familiar with PTSD and had conducted numerous Critical Incident Stress Debriefings for first responders and veterans in my community. Yet, I didn't recognize that it was sneaking up on me.

In 2003 a little girl who attended our Sunday school suffered a terrible tragedy. She was stomped to death by her stepmother. This event would be the catalyst which opened my eyes to my struggle with PTSD. I did not recognize the little girl's name, so I went to the funeral home to see who it was. When I walked in, I immediately smelled a terrible stench of death—just like the Morgue at Ground Zero. Somehow, I managed to go through with the process of seeing her lifeless body. When I saw her, I did remember who she was. Later, I recalled how she loved to show Pastor Jim how pretty her dress looked, or to tell me what story she heard in Sunday school.

But I don't remember anything that happened immediately after that. The next thing I remember is sort of coming to myself and finding that I was in the middle of a farmer's field. I was twenty miles away from the location of the funeral home, and I had my engine running. I was completely unable to recall driving there, and I had no idea why I might have come there.

My face hurt, and I could tell it was from crying. My throat and body physically ached from screaming and pounding the steering wheel. Honestly, if someone had walked up to the car at that point, they would have called the police and assumed that I was a madman.

Another time, I was trying to unwind by doing something I love: fly fishing. After hiking to a spot on the river that looked promising, I started to assemble the fly rod. With seemingly no trigger of any kind, I began shaking, crying, and feeling like I needed to vomit. It was very troubling to me that I could not connect these feelings to anything about my location or activities.

It was only on my climb back to the car that I finally figured out what had triggered the bizarre response. On my way down to the river, I had passed a dead animal in the bushes and the stink of death brought it all back. No one who knew me would have ever assumed this sort of thing was happening to me. I didn't tell anyone because I was ashamed that I hadn't gotten past 'the 9/11 stuff' yet.

One incident, however, really got my attention and helped me to see that I couldn't solve this problem on my own. I was at the golf course and I had made it a practice to be the last one to tee off at the end of the day. However on this particular evening there was a bevy of activity. I assumed that a tournament must have been wrapping up.

Looking up, I noticed at least five golf carts driving in circuitous routes and zigzagging across the course. "Oh great," I thought. "This must be a bunch of guys who have been partying."

Then the man from the pro shop filled me in on what was happening. "Those are cops and volunteers. There was a tournament today and one guy is pretty sure he lost his loaded revolver somewhere on the course. They're driving around to look for it." I am ashamed to report what happened next. For just a few moments, I had a very dark thought cross my mind —I hoped I would find the revolver.

The very next day I went to the VA hospital and sought help for PTSD.

THE COMFORTER SENDS COMFORT AGAIN

Around that same time—when I realized I was struggling terribly from PTSD—I got a call from one of the moms in our church. Her little girl was in the pediatric unit at a hospital in Springfield and asked if I would go visit her. I was glad to do it. After visiting the girl, I came out into the hallway, and there in the hall, staring up at me was a German Shepherd.

"Bruno?" I asked, looking straight at the dog.

He came right to me. I looked at his owner, but it was not the person I remembered from 9/11. Still, somehow I knew that this was the same dog.

I turned to the owner and just asked, "Ground Zero?"

She told me that yes, the dog had been at Ground Zero. It was Bruno! We sat and visited and I enjoyed Bruno's company for a good while. There are no words to describe the effect that seeing Bruno again had on me in that moment. From the moment I first saw him, I was acutely aware that the Lord was showing me two things. First, He was letting me know that He has perfect, intimate knowledge of the struggle that was going on inside of me. Second, He was showing me that He was with me—that He was willing and able to help me get through it all.

What are the odds of randomly running into Bruno again all those years later, all the way on the other side of the country? In case anyone is still skeptical, believing that this was some kind of incredibly rare coincidence, the Lord would see to it that I would have one more encounter that involved Bruno—seventeen years after 9/11.

In 2018, my sister was dying. Joan is an amazing person, one of the kindest, most sincere individuals I have ever met. Throughout her life she loved the Lord, and even as she was dying, she was witnessing to anyone who would listen. She and I spoke almost every week. She endured my preacher stories and prayed with me during my dark times, and I did the same in hers. Now she was dying, and I was preparing to go back to be with her in Florida.

I was needing to shop for some things for my trip. Though there was a store 15 minutes away, I decided to take a drive in the country, and ended up in a neighboring town 20 miles away. There was a Starbucks next to the store where I did my shopping. It was a warm day, and many people were sitting outside under umbrellas, enjoying their coffee. On the way in, I spotted a lady with a German Shepherd. He was smaller than I remembered Bruno being, but I did think of Bruno for a second. Then I quickly brushed aside the thought, sure that Bruno was gone by now.

My usual response when I come across someone walking their dog is to ask the owner's permission to say hello to their four-legged friend. Often, I would then tell them about the dogs at Ground Zero, and what heroic animals they were. This time, for some reason, I didn't go over to them. I remember thinking "People don't want to hear that stuff anymore . . . it's been so long ago now."

So, I walked on by, then went inside and ordered my coffee. On my way out, I couldn't help myself and went over to the lady and her dog. "Is it okay if I say hi to your dog?" She smiled and gave her consent. I extended my hand for the dog to sniff, and then patted his head. I told her why I loved dogs so much, and what they did at Ground Zero. Then I told her the story about Bruno.

What happened next really boggled my mind.

"Oh, you must mean *Uno*. Uno was at Ground Zero."

Uno poses with medical personnel in the V-MET tent at Ground Zero on September 27th, 2001. Photo by Michael Rieger, FEMA News

After all these years, it turns out I had the dog's name wrong. The lady went on to tell me the entire history of Uno's blood line. This dog I was seeing at Starbuck's was one of Uno's descendants.

Coincidence? Twice?

Again, in that moment, the Holy Spirit was showing me that His comfort is always available—that He is deeply and compassionately interested in our griefs and sorrows.

Jesus said something profound to His disciples on the night before he went to the cross: "I will ask the Father, and he will give you another Helper, to be with you forever, even the Spirit of truth, whom the world cannot receive, because it neither sees him nor knows him. You know him, for he dwells with you and will be in you. I will not leave you as orphans; I will come to you" (John 14:15-18 ESV).

Jesus promises those who know Him that He will never leave them. He has sent His Helper, the Holy Spirit, to comfort us in all of our troubles.

10

ESCORTING FAMILY MEMBERS TO GROUND ZERO

"Yea, though I walk through the valley of the
shadow of death, I will fear no evil: for
thou art with me."

— PSALM 23:4 KJV

WHEN THE FERRY arrived near Wall Street, our group made its way to the staging area. The people on the street soon figured out who we were and where we were headed. Everyone stopped talking and bowed their heads. Many covered their hearts.

I have often thought back to that day—what a kind gesture this was. It reminded me of a custom still observed in some rural areas. When a funeral procession goes by, people pull off to the side of the road, get out of their cars, hold their hands over their hearts, and bow their heads to show respect. Brokers and traders from Wall Street who were on their breaks stopped what they were doing and bowed their heads as our sad procession made its way to the Pile.

The City of New York had decided to offer family members who lost loved ones the opportunity to see Ground Zero. This was about midway through my time at Ground Zero. A staging area was prepared and families were ferried, fifty at a time, to a spot near Wall Street. Accompanied by chaplains and mental health workers, the family members would disembark, and walk about an eighth of a mile to see where their loved ones perished.

MAYOR GIULIANI IS CHALLENGED

I remember that first trip well. In a curtained-off area, 50 family members sat in rows. Dr. Grace Telesco, the Mayor's point person for assisting the families, gave a brief talk, explaining to the family members what they were about to experience. Her handling of such a delicate situation was stellar, so much so that our team of chaplains later gave her the nickname, "Amazing Grace."

Dr. Telesco introduced the chaplains and other counselors who would be accompanying them to Ground Zero. Then she said words to this effect. "There is one other group I want to introduce. They have traveled here at their own expense because they felt that they, of all people, might be able to relate with how you are feeling right now."

Then she introduced the group—most of them had traveled all the way from Oklahoma City just to be with the families. Each one of them had lost a family member when the Alfred P. Murrah building was destroyed. It was as if a giant, warm blanket descended on the room.

Now it was time for me to start meeting the family members. Apprehensive, I prayed that I would not say anything trite or harmful to any of these traumatized people. I have learned over the years that it is the nervous banter that can wound people and that sometimes it is best to be silent. So I tried not to say very much as we walked.

When we got to Ground Zero, there was a sound unlike anything I had ever heard—something akin to a scream, a sob, and muffled unintelligible moans all rolled into one. When the family members finally laid eyes on the site, many of them fainted. More than a few of them vomited. One lady pulled out tufts of her hair till her scalp bled.

I made note of one man and made it my business to stay close to him. As we disembarked from the ferry and began walking through Wall Street I thought to myself, *This man looks like a heart attack waiting to happen.* With the Pile as his backdrop, Giuliani faced the families and told them he wasn't going to talk much, but that he would try and get them oriented as to what they were looking at. He pointed, "That is where Tower One was . . ."

The man I was concerned about began to breathe hard and get extremely agitated. He began to move toward the Mayor, increasingly raising his voice. He yelled "This is all your fault . . . This is all your fault . . . My son is dead . . . It's your fault!" Before I knew what happened I had grabbed one of the man's arms and Giuliani had the other. We were holding him up and Giuliani was patting the man's chest saying, "I'm so sorry about your son."

On the ferry boat ride back, Mayor Giuliani came over to me, grabbed my hands, and stared into my face for what felt like a long time. Then he said, "Thank you for coming here to help us." This would not be the last time that someone would stare at my face like that.

HELPING THE HURTING

From that day on, we would take the ferry numerous times each day, 50 at a time; our precious cargo—the grieving loved ones of the victims of 9/11. Many of those ferry trips stick out in my memory.

One day we heard that there was going to be a special ferry just for United Airlines personnel based in New York. They came in their uniforms. Keep in mind these were colleagues and friends of the crew from the ill-fated United flight that the terrorists used as a live bomb by crashing it into the South Tower. After staring at the smoldering ruins in disbelief, they huddled together. One of them pulled out what appeared to be a rolled-up sign or banner. Facing the recovery workers, crane operators, firefighters, and cops, they unfurled it.

I sensed this was a holy moment, so I didn't even attempt to read what was written. I learned later that the banner was created to thank all of the recovery workers for their efforts to locate the United employees' fallen comrades. I vividly recall one crane operator who, when he saw it, climbed down from his machine and wept like a baby.

On another trip, I was with a group of four siblings whose mother had perished. I began my talk with them, "We are going to travel by ferry, get off, and then walk to the staging area prepared for you. This will be the hardest trip you ever make. If I may, I would like to be with you. I also want to ask your permission to do something before we come back."

When they saw 'the Pile' they collapsed into a group hug —weeping and trembling. After what seemed like a long time, our leader started to steer us back to the ferry. I told them, "Remember, I asked your permission to ask you to do something before we came back?" They nodded their assent.

I said, "I watched the pain and horror on your faces as you stared at all this destruction. Now I am going to ask you to look just once more—only this time, I want you to look away from the Pile and look up at the crane operators, the dog handlers, and the construction workers who are expressing their condolences and offering comfort to you, as they look for your mom."

Almost as if on cue, an exhausted, filthy, sooty recovery worker stared right at them. Then he took off his hard hat and covered his heart. They grabbed me and heaved sobs and told me they would never forget. I knew I would never forget either.

On another day, I accompanied a lady who had come up to me with a request. She asked that when we got to the Pile, would I please take her to the 'man in charge'? She had to know there was no hope, yet she clung to the idea that she could personally direct the rescuers to where her husband worked. "I know they are looking in the wrong place. I can show them. I can show them."

When she finally made her way up to the Pile, she slumped to her knees. The look of utter horror and bewilderment on her face is etched in my memory.

"They're never going to find him, are they?"

I asked her if it would be alright if I prayed. I knelt with her and prayed, "Lord you know where he is. Let this dear woman find where You are. Comfort her by your Holy Spirit, Oh God."

The next trip had me concerned for one young man on board. He was a 20-something with his gaze fixed, his hands clenched, sitting rigidly like a piece of cardboard. I sat next to him and he did not flinch, move, or acknowledge that he could even hear me. I said to him, "I am not going to talk. I have made this trip with lots of family members and if it's okay with you, I'm going to walk with you and stand by you."

When he saw the Pile he clenched his fists even tighter. His face contorted into a grimace. He opened his mouth as if to scream but nothing came out. I have seen this before with traumatized veterans: the silent scream.

I propped him up and steered him back to the ferry. His gaze never changed. When we rode back to the pier, I still felt that I should say nothing, but just be with him. Then what almost seemed like "the Angel of the Lord" appeared, but it was actually a golden retriever.

This beautiful four-legged comforter came over and put his head on the man's lap. He turned his eyes to the young man, who was too traumatized to respond. Then I saw a miracle. The man's fist relaxed, and his pinkie finger touched the dog's fur. His gaze still fixed, he allowed more of his hand to relax. He began to stroke the dog's head. Tears appeared at the corners of his eyes.

This dog had definitely been a godsend.

The man's body, no longer rigid, began to relax. He gave out a low guttural sound, then a sob. Then he began to convulsively weep and wail. I put my arms around him, and he wept for quite a while. Then he finally confessed his pain, "It was my fiancée—we were going to be married next week."

THE FERRYMAN

My last memory of the ferry rides involved another Holy Spirit arranged encounter. Getting around Manhattan was a real case of adapting and overcoming. As I mentioned, our team of chaplains was blessed to have a 12-passenger van and a driver. Each day we traveled from Staten Island to the Pile for three hours, then to the Morgue for three hours, and finally to the pier buildings where the families were being cared for.

There were occasions, however, when other conveyances were necessary, such as the rental car I used on my drive to the Coast Guard Cutter. Another time, I had to get from point A to point B, and flagged down a unique Coast Guard vessel appropriately named *Thunder One*. It was, I assume, used in drug interdiction missions. My New England chaplain colleagues would describe it as 'wicked fast.' I remember the crew smiling as they told me to button up, cover my eyes, and keep my mouth shut. When they got underway, the boat went so fast we were airborne at some points. I'm sure I provided some comic relief for the crew, as I dug my fingernails into the seat and held on for dear life.

One day after the last group of families returned to the pier, I needed to get back to the rendezvous point so I could take the van back to where we were billeted. By this point I had gotten comfortable with flagging down cop cars or any official-looking vehicle to ask for a ride.

Looking around, I saw that the empty ferry was getting ready to leave. I jumped on and bummed a ride. A few crew members were securing for the day, and I saw a man in the wheelhouse. I took the liberty of striking up a conversation with him. I asked the man how he was doing before moving on to deeper topics.

"So, were you on duty that day?"

His demeanor changed. "Yes," he said with sorrow in his voice.

As you will no doubt remember, thousands of New Yorkers fled on foot across the bridges while the Twin Towers were on fire. My niece, I would later learn, was in that mass of people. What you may not have seen on the television news coverage is that as many, or perhaps even more people, fled to the sea wall. This ferry captain's vessel, like anything that floated, was called into service to evacuate people from Manhattan. The activity on the water that day quickly became the largest maritime evacuation in the history of the United States.

It became immediately clear to this man and his crew that they would have to get out and go call people—directing them to the ferry. They, like all of the heroic first responders, ran toward the burning towers as thousands ran away. As he recalled that morning, I saw it again. *The stare.* He looked almost as if he were in a trance. In slow motion, he turned his eyes up and began describing the jumpers who landed on the pavement near him. As he described this event to me, his eyes slowly went through the motion of following the jumpers' fall from the towers, until finally his eyes came to rest, pointed all the way down at the deck.

He was seeing it again.

This man had been there for the event, and was now ferrying family members back to Ground Zero everyday, where they would relive the nightmare for themselves.

Heroically, the ferryman would hold back his own sorrow and see the mourners safely back.

Such were the heroes of New York.

The sequence of people reliving that day—where they were, what they were doing—repeated itself in front of me numerous times while I was in New York. Giuliani had seen jumpers too. So did the staff of the Medical Examiner's office and the Port Authority workers, the cops, the firefighters, and just about anyone who was in or around the World Trade Center that day. Still, somehow these same individuals found a way to not only keep doing their jobs, but to do so in a professional manner.

My job was to be with them, and in so doing, to show them that the One called "the Comforter" was with them too. I prayed for the ferryman as I hopped off to meet our team. Whenever the anniversary comes around, I always remember him.

And I always will.

THE CROSS IN THE PILE

For the message of the cross is foolishness to those who are perishing, but to us who are being saved it is the power of God.

— 1 CORINTHIANS 1:18 NIV

YOU CAN DRIVE on any road in America and periodically pass little makeshift memorials people set up on the shoulder. Some have plastic flowers. Perhaps a teddy bear or a photograph. And almost always, a cross.

The cross is also a favorite tattoo, often sported by people who claim no religious affiliation or belief system. The cross is a powerful image which brings out the strongest of emotions.

In our current cancel-culture nightmare, statues and memorials and anything to do with the image of the cross is not only a matter of debate, but often the subject of demonstrations and protests.

In the summer of 2020, Oregon was under siege. The mob of "mostly peaceful protestors" was, in reality, infiltrated by rioters who are anything but peaceful. Seattle, Portland, and Eugene are all places where first responders, the police, fire, and EMS personnel were being assaulted with chunks of concrete, bricks, pipes, rebar, bags of feces, and bags of urine —all of which were strategically hidden by 'protestors' in advance of their event.

Businesses were destroyed. Lives were lost. All the while, local and state politicians did nothing to stem the tide, and in some cases actually encouraged the lawlessness.

As a pastor, I was forbidden to see an elderly patient in a nursing home, due ostensibly to public health concerns, yet thousands of rioters could spit in the faces of police with impunity. The shameless politicians claimed that the "mostly peaceful" demonstrators have their right to protest but churches were singled out for draconian isolation measures. Forbidden to sing praises to God. Think about that.

As it turned out, the mob in Eugene was coming for the cross.

CROSS IN THE CROSSHAIRS

For over a decade, I had the privilege to teach at the Eugene Bible College, which now goes by the name of New Hope Christian College. Recently, a former student contacted me and shared news reports that a mob of "mostly peaceful protestors" is coming after the 50-foot cross which used to be a landmark in the City of Eugene. Some people claim that this cross was a "KKK cross" but that is completely false.[1]

Originally donated and erected by a private donor in 1964, City of Eugene citizens voted by a wide margin in 1970 to officially designate the cross as a memorial to United States war veterans. In 1997 it was moved from its lofty site on Skinner's Butte to the campus of New Hope.

Why was it moved there? The 9th Circuit Court of Appeals ruled that the cross violated the First Amendment. The college graciously stepped up and offered their campus to house the cultural landmark. 23 years after it was relocated, Antifa announced their plans on Facebook: They were coming for the cross.

After reading about the controversy, I decided to drive to the campus in advance of the event, paying careful attention to park my car far away and walk to the college, as many of the "mostly peaceful" demonstrators in Portland and Eugene had been trashing and burning cars.

Hiking a mile or so, I got to the campus, which sits on a 20-acre site with a commanding view of the city of Eugene. It was a little unsettling seeing a security checkpoint set up so that vehicles couldn't pull close to the buildings. I was heartened, though, to see that others seemed to have had the same prompting I did: Just show up and pray.

There were 300 others who had done the exact same thing!

The cross itself is mounted in an amphitheater at the center of the campus. I felt that I was to walk around the perimeter and just pray in the Spirit. Later a team of students led us all in a sustained time of praise and worship. The President of the college then gave what I felt was a measured summary of the facts of the threat, and then had us extend our hands toward the city below and pray for the Governor, the Mayor, and law enforcement agents. Then we prayed for the protestors! I distinctly remember him praying that they wouldn't even show up.

They never did. I later heard that the state police stopped two busloads of Antifa activists on the interstate that night. That same weekend, Antifa agitators did manage to burn Bibles and American flags in front of the federal courthouse in Portland.[2]

But for now at least, the cross still stands.

All that night I reflected on the phenomenon of crosses being removed all over America. I remembered that President Obama insisted that the chapel at Georgetown cover a cross that would have otherwise been visible as he spoke.[3] Many military chapels no longer have crosses. VA facilities have strict guidelines about crosses and the lack thereof. I remember when General Schwarzkopf decided that his chaplains in Desert Storm were not to wear crosses.

But then I remembered at least one place where the presence of a cross had not been protested. Anne Bybee grabbed a disposable camera and captured the moment when God brought a sense of peace to an otherwise dark scene at Ground Zero.

Photo of "The Cross at the Pile" taken by Anne Bybee

A BEACON OF HOPE

Anne Bybee was at Ground Zero to help provide logistical support to medical and rescue workers who were working at the Pile. In that capacity, Anne worked very long days at the Pile, and after a while, she began to feel overwhelmed by what she was seeing.

Just about the time she was feeling desperate for some kind of hope, Anne looked up and saw something that she felt was a sign from God. Emerging from the rubble was a cross made from two sections of I-beam.

Twisted and leaning to one side, the Ground Zero cross reminds us that God Himself is hurt by human tragedy. He feels emotions. He feels pain.

Yet, He did not leave us here alone.

Jesus chose to step down out of Heaven, and come take

part in human pain. He chose to experience the pain of loss and death for Himself, as a human being. When we hurt, He hurts. That's what love does. If you love someone, you will hurt when they hurt. And God desperately loves all of humanity.

I had the chance to speak with Anne about her experience and her photo, and she graciously gave us permission to use it for our book. Anne says that the cross gave her a sense of peace, of knowing that God was present in the midst of tragedy. I am grateful to Anne for her service and for persevering through the pain long enough to capture this beautiful reminder that our Savior is always present with us in our pain. Thank you, Anne.

There was another, similar discovery that took place at the Pile. Frank Silecchia, an excavation worker from New York, worked in early search and rescue efforts. After a long day of searching, they had found three bodies, and Silecchia was exhausted. But he felt an urge to keep going, and he pressed through to another section of the Pile.

Coming to somewhat of an opening, he looked up and saw multiple steel crosses, with the largest one being about 20 feet. He described that moment in an article he wrote for Guideposts magazine.[4]

In that little grotto I felt a strange sense of peace and stillness. I could almost hear God saying, *The terrible thing done at this site was meant for evil. But I will turn it to good. Have faith. I am here.* I fell to my knees in front of the largest cross. Tears came, and I couldn't stop them. I cried like a baby.

— FRANK SILECCHIA, 9/11 RESCUE
WORKER

Frank spray painted the words, "God's House" in that area of the Pile, and he would sometimes go back there to renew his strength. I also appreciated Mr. Silecchia's honesty about the response of others who saw "God's House." Some had a very similar reaction to his own. Others didn't notice it or feel it had any significance.

But many did feel that the cross was very important, so they fought to save it once the cleanup work required that section to be disturbed. A priest friend of Silecchia, Father Brian Jordan, got involved and along with others, was able to persuade officials to save the large 20-foot cross. They got an expedited approval from Mayor Giuliani to erect the cross atop a concrete pedestal at Ground Zero—in constant view of rescue workers. The large cross ended up being the one that was largely referred to as the "Ground Zero Cross."

Ground Zero Cross (cropped version) Original Photo by Samuel Li

I can only give my personal testimony of the effect that cross had on the workers at the Pile. There was a definite buzz about the cross once it was moved to the concrete pedestal. That's when a lot of people first began to hear about it and see it.

"Did you hear about it?"

"Have you seen it?"

"You won't believe what some guy found."

There was a renewed vigor, and finally, something good to talk about, even if only for a few minutes. The cross is a reminder that death is not the end—that through Jesus Christ, eternal life is available to us. Because He lives, we can live too.

I confess that when I first saw it at Ground Zero, I thought about why the cross is such a polarizing symbol. It offends people because it is also a reminder that there is a cost to sin —that God is holy and just, and He cannot just overlook sin. Sin has to be dealt with. Justice has to be done.

I can still remember the construction workers looking up at the cross and taking off their hard hats, covering their hearts, and bowing their heads. Many were making the sign of the cross. I believe there would have been a reaction of anger and indignation had the City of New York tried to take that cross out while the police and fire community were digging for the remains of their comrades.

As it happened though, the cross remained during the cleanup phase, and was moved into storage for a time during reconstruction, before finding its final resting place in the National September 11 Memorial & Museum in New York.

HOW SOON WE FORGET

So much has transpired in the 20 years since 9/11.

When I returned to Oregon after my stint at the Pile, I purposed that I would put together a service in Cottage Grove, Oregon, to honor all of the first responders who served our city. That service remains one of the most memorable of my entire ministry. Mayors and police chiefs, city council members, and county commissioners stood to their feet as we applauded uniformed officers from the fire department and law enforcement. There were local, county, state, and federal officers present.

Veterans' organizations marched in and lined the 600-seat auditorium. In my message that day, I made it a point to tell those in attendance about the cross at the Pile, and how indebted we are to these special people who are the first responders when bad things happen.

As we near the 20th anniversary, here in Oregon, police are now treated like dirt. A service like the one we had in 2002 couldn't happen today without provoking a dangerous confrontation. We would need security to protect the police.

The remarks I made at that service to honor law enforcement might very well land me in jail for hate speech if I made them today. What will our ultimate destination be if we continue in all of this hatred and division?

During the prayer meeting at New Hope Bible College—when protestors were said to be coming for the cross—I saw something that I cannot unsee. At the same school where I had years before taught fledgling ministers, there were now armed men with high-powered rifles on the roof. They were there to provide security for those in the amphitheater where the cross was located.

LEARNING FROM HISTORY

In 2014, my book, *Fatal Drift: Is the Church Losing Its Anchor?*, was released. In a chapter titled, "The Offence of the Cross," I quoted Pastor Erwin W. Lutzer, Pastor Emeritus of The Moody Church in Chicago, Illinois. In 1995, Lutzer had written an important book titled, *Hitler's Cross: The Story of How the Cross of Christ was Used as a Symbol of the Nazi*

Agenda. I remember the looks I got from fellow pastors when I told them the title of Lutzer's book. A few of them rolled their eyes as if to say, "Come on, that's conspiracy theory stuff!"

Some of these same self-identified "progressive pastors" were the first ones to start to downplay the Bible and to bend their teachings to accommodate the postmodern influence which was sweeping through synods and seminaries. Lutzer described the debate among German clergy regarding what the church should do about the Nazis.

> The church stood poised between two crosses, wanting to be loyal to both but learning that neither could tolerate the other. The church made peace with an enemy with which it should have been at war. Called to warn and protect, it tolerated, then saluted, then submitted.
>
> — PASTOR ERWIN LUTZER

The cross is always a point of division—it separates. Trying to downplay the significance of the cross by devaluing the Bible does not strip the cross of its power. If anything, that will only make the dividing line more sharp and more clear. Just like the Germans had a decision to make—they could choose the true cross of Christ or the false cross of Hitler— America has a similar choice.

Some Christians have taken the wrong course. The more they drift from the sound doctrine of the Bible, the more they end up teaching a false gospel. As a result, their churches are stripped of the life-changing power of the true Gospel.

Inexplicably, what we've seen so far is that they have a

tendency to double down on their false ideas rather than turning back to the true Gospel. As Lutzer pointed out, the church in Germany "mistook the temporal benefits of the swastika for the spiritual benefits of the cross of Christ. Wanting to believe that Hitler was the answer, it forgot what the important questions were."[5]

In 2020, Erwin Lutzer wrote another prophetic warning to the American Church. He titled it, *We Will Not Be Silenced: Responding Courageously to Our Culture's Assault on Christianity.*

As I read Lutzer's latest book, I recalled the rubble of Ground Zero. The sad convoy of dump trucks heading to Fresh Kills. The grim scene of first responders and forensic experts sifting through shards from the shattered dreams of a generation. Erwin Lutzer raises yet again the fact that we are too easily seduced by the notion that the mission of the church is synonymous with the propaganda of warmed-over, repackaged, 'new and improved' Marxism that is rapidly taking over our national life.

But Marxism is not the answer. Though it promises a utopian society, it has never solved any problem. No matter how it gets repackaged, socialism has never brought about any good for humankind—only pain, destruction, and evil. In spite of that clear and undeniable fact, many in America seem to be running headfirst into the snake pit of communism.

There is another answer.

We would do well to remember the words of an old hymn:[6]

There's room at the cross for you

There's room at the cross for you
Though millions have come,
There's still room for one
Yes, there's room at the cross for you

— IRA STANPHILL

I HAVE SEEN THE ENEMY

For our struggle is not against flesh and blood, but against the rulers, against the authorities, against the powers of this dark world and against the spiritual forces of evil in the heavenly realms

— EPHESIANS 6:12 NIV

IN THE IMMEDIATE aftermath of the attacks of September 11th, pundits, pastors, and prognosticators all claimed to know the reasons why America was attacked. Some facts were obvious. For the terrorists, it was a matter of "justifiable Jihad." The tension had been mounting for many years. Who could forget the spectacle in Tehran when American Hostages were paraded before cameras as mobs chanted "death to the Great Satan"?

Virtually every Friday, from mosques in Iran and around the world, the chants continued. "Death to America! Death to the Great Satan!" According to Osama Bin Laden, the immediate rationale for the animus towards America was the presence of U.S. troops in areas deemed to be Islamic holy sites. Bin Laden had spent years amassing power for himself in Jihadist circles, and once he had consolidated his power, he declared a Fatwa against America.

A NEED TO IDENTIFY THE ENEMY

In the years following 9/11, I was afforded the opportunity to teach seminary courses and one of the classes I developed was *Crisis Ministry*. Drawing from my experience at Ground Zero and other events that were deemed to be "critical incidents," I put together a syllabus designed to educate local church pastors and leaders. It was geared toward those who wanted to prepare for the role of helping first responders in their communities, should a crisis arise there.

There were great sources of information to draw on when I put together the course. From events like the Oklahoma City bombing, to 9/11, to Hurricane Katrina, research done by Drs. Jeff Mitchell and George Everly have revolutionized the way we process traumatic events. Mitchell and Everly introduced the now gold standard "Critical Incident Stress Debriefing" techniques used to help first responders deal with traumatic events. The reading list for my course included articles and books from their organization, which is called the Critical Incident Stress Foundation.

In 2002, I was invited to conduct a modular version of this class in Chicago. On the final day of class, I conducted a mock debriefing to demonstrate the efficacy of the technique. For our "critical incident," I picked a scenario that I knew everyone would be able to relate to—a fictional bombing of the Sears Tower in Chicago.

Students were assigned different roles to play, such as emergency room nurse, firefighter, police officer, and dispatcher. Before the mock debriefing, I gave a detailed description of the stages of the Critical Incident Debriefing process. As soon as I began to describe what we were about to do, one lady became visibly agitated. She got up and began to pace back and forth at the back of the room.

I said, "If you are uncomfortable with this, by all means, you don't have to participate in this exercise. If you want to go into the break room and grab a cup of coffee that's fine."

By this point, her whole demeanor changed and she was breathing hard "No, I have to do this," she said as she rejoined the group. I got her a glass of water.

Initially, each of the participants went around the circle and identified themselves and their roles on the day of the (hypothetical) bombing. This was the *fact phase*. Next, we came to the *thought phase*. This is the phase in the debriefing where I asked the participants: "At the end of that first day (our imagined bombing of the Sears Tower) when you finally had time to process what had happened—when you went off autopilot so to say—what was your first thought?"

My agitated friend went first. Her body language indicated that she was reliving a painful event and *her stare* was something I had seen many times before at the Pile. "I knew it was Muslims," she said. Her classmates exchanged puzzled looks. I'm so glad I didn't speak immediately. I just waited. Then she told her story.

Back in 1992, she worked as a driver for a bus company that offered tours of the Windy City. One of her assignments was to take children from a Muslim school to see the sights in Chicago. She made numerous trips with these kids that year and developed a warm relationship with them.

One day the kids were all excited. They explained, "A very famous preacher is coming to our Mosque. Won't you come and listen to him?" She agreed to come but knew she would have some cultural hurdles to deal with. She was not a Muslim, and she was a woman. She was, however, allowed to remotely listen.

She was sweating now—her voice quivering as she continued her story. "Five minutes into his sermon, I was horrified. I left and immediately contacted the FBI office in Chicago and reported what I heard. This man was calling for violence against the infidel, the Great Satan—America! In chilling detail, he openly declared what he deemed were Allah's plans for striking America."

Most shocking to her was the response she received from the FBI. They already knew about him. He was on their radar. They were monitoring his sermons. They thanked her for calling and she never heard from them again. The famous preacher? He was none other than Omar Abdel-Rahman, the so-called "Blind Sheikh" who was later convicted for his role in the 1993 World Trade Center bombing. He was responsible for a plot to bomb major NYC landmarks, tunnels, and the United Nations building.

Almost 10 years after her experience, my crisis ministry student assumed that if the Sears Tower had been bombed, the perpetrators—the enemy—would be Muslim extremists. The failure of the authorities to act on her testimony about the Blind Sheikh had troubled her deeply for the next 10 years or so after the incident.

Even after he was imprisoned for life, the Blind Sheikh continued to hold great influence with his disciples. In 2012, a group calling themselves "The Brigades of the Imprisoned Sheikh Omar Abdul Rahman" claimed responsibility for the bombing of the U.S. Consulate in Bengazi, Libya.[1]

As I looked back on that incident in 2002, I thought of a term used by pastoral counselors, "the identified patient." A couple, family, or group present themselves to a counselor for help. Eventually, one of those people in particular would be referred to in the counselor's notes as "the identified patient." The thinking among professional counselors was that the entire family obviously had serious issues, but there is one who is put forth by the rest of the group as "the one who needs to be fixed" in counseling. The person receives the designation of the *identified* patient. They're all patients, but one of them is being identified by the group as the "real" patient.

That terminology can be borrowed to explain my purpose for including a discussion of the enemy in a book about 9/11. Let's call him the "Identified Enemy." There are a host of reasons behind the 9/11 attacks, but when something that traumatic takes place, there is an immediate need for a narrative that identifies *the* enemy.

So, who was "the" enemy on 9/11? If you had asked Osama Bin Laden, who issued the Fatwah against America, he would have said it was the American government for violating the holy sites of Islam and for its support of Israel. If you had asked the Bush administration, they would have unequivocally answered that the enemy was "radical Islam"— in particular, Osama Bin Laden and Al Qaeda. In short order though, the enemy label would be extended to Saddam

Hussein. It wasn't long at all before the "War on Terror" expanded its parameters, and a new cast of characters were tagged with the *enemy* moniker.

THE ENEMY OF OUR SOULS

Being an eyewitness to the handiwork of the diabolical people who slaughtered thousands of innocent people on 9/11—and being a Christian minister—my choice for an enemy to blame was the devil. There is something about the heartless massacre of innocents throughout history that forensically fits the scriptural profile of the devil.

The murder of baby Hebrew boys in Egypt.

The rape of Nanking.

The murder of baby boys in Bethlehem.

The planned purges of millions upon millions in China and Russia.

And perhaps the most singularly Satanic horror of all—the Holocaust.

These types of events seem to somehow hint that the monsters who perpetrated them were empowered and enabled by a malevolent spirit giving supernatural support to accomplish carnage at such a global level. If it wasn't the devil directly—and it rarely is—I can say confidently that the scriptures portray Satan as the behind-the-scenes puppet master, pulling the strings, crafting the lies, and fueling the atrocities.

Another clue that the devil had a hand in the 9/11 attacks is how methodical and heartless it all was. Hitler, Stalin, and Mao paid nutritionists to advise them on how to slowly starve millions while continuing to exploit them as slave laborers.

Great care and intricate logistical support were required to execute the Final Solution. A methodical, patient plan was years in the making. And somehow, Satan is very good at making the perpetrators of evil believe that the ones being murdered are the ones who are actually evil.

The attack on the so-called "Great Satan" was no less calculated, methodically planned, and executed. The length of time spent planning the attacks on September 11th. The pilot training. The metallurgical studies on how long it would take jet fuel to melt steel. Which way the towers would topple. How many thousands would be vaporized. Rehearsing how to slit throats with box cutters. It was all planned out, step by step, piece by piece.

In the devil, we have an adversary who has a long-term perspective in mind. He thinks in terms of how to affect generations. I remember an encounter I had with a chaplain at one of our conferences. While conducting our devotions that morning, I had cited a few references from the Bible, one of which mentioned the devil. This chaplain, with an advanced theological degree and at least a decade of public ministry under his belt, got me aside later that day and said, "So, do you mean to tell me that you believe that there is an actual, real, personal devil?"

"And you mean to tell me that you don't?" I replied.

I believe it was C.S. Lewis who taught that "the most effective trick the devil has is to convince people that he doesn't exist." Lewis also wrote in *The Screwtape Letters*, "The greatest evil is not done now in sordid dens of crime. It is not even done in concentration camps and labor camps. In those, we see its result. But [the greatest evil] is conceived and ordered—moved, seconded, and carried and minuted—in clear, carpeted, warmed, and well-lit offices, by quiet men with white collars and cut fingernails and smooth-shaven cheeks who do not need to raise their voice."

Probably the second most toxic narrative the devil puts forth is that God doesn't want us to be fulfilled and happy—but he (Satan) does. At the very beginning of the world, in the Garden of Eden, the serpent tempted Eve with the very first words of Satan ever recorded on earth:

> The Lord God took the man and put him in the Garden of Eden to work it and take care of it. And the Lord God commanded the man, "You are free to eat from any tree in the garden; but you must not eat from the tree of the knowledge of good and evil, for when you eat from it you will certainly die."
>
> — GENESIS 2:15-17 NIV

> Now the serpent was more crafty than any of the wild animals the Lord God had made. He said to the woman, "Did God really say, 'You must not eat from any tree in the garden'?"

> The woman said to the serpent, "We may eat fruit from the trees in the garden, but God did say, 'You must not eat fruit from the tree that is in the middle of the garden, and you must not touch it, or you will die.'"

> **"You will not certainly die,"** the serpent said to the woman. **"For God knows that when you eat from it your**

eyes will be opened, and you will be like God, knowing good and evil."

— GENESIS 3:1-5 NIV

Another one of the seminary courses I taught over the years was titled Prison Epistles. One of the Apostle Paul's letters from prison was addressed to the church at Ephesus. In this important letter, he reminds the Ephesians that there are some matters with cosmic implications that coincide with the affairs of men on earth.

Finally, be strong in the Lord and in his mighty power. Put on the full armor of God, so that you can take your stand against the devil's schemes. For our struggle is not against flesh and blood, but against the rulers, against the authorities, against the powers of this dark world and against the spiritual forces of evil in the heavenly realms. Therefore put on the full armor of God, so that when the day of evil comes, you may be able to stand your ground, and after you have done everything, to stand.

— EPHESIANS 6:10-13 NIV

The Greek word that gets translated as "schemes" there is *methodeias*, which is the same root word we use to get 'methods,' 'methodical,' and 'methodologies.' The devil has methods and schemes that he uses against human beings. He's methodical. He plans out a course of action to take in an effort to divide and destroy human beings.

The Apostle Peter wrote to believers in Asia Minor to warn of the persecution that was coming their way.

Humble yourselves, therefore, under God's mighty hand, that he may lift you up in due time. Cast all your anxiety on him because he cares for you.

Be alert and of sober mind. Your enemy the devil prowls around like a roaring lion looking for someone to devour. Resist him, standing firm in the faith, because you know that the family of believers throughout the world is undergoing the same kind of sufferings.

— 1 PETER 5:6-9 NIV

SATAN'S PUBLIC RELATIONS FIRM

As I considered these biblical truths about Satan, I thought back to the late 1960s and the early 1970s. It was during that period that I was born again and began to pay attention to the Bible. Also at that time, there were very popular books with titles like *The Late, Great Planet Earth*, and *Satan is Alive and Well.*

In 60s pop culture, rock music began to take on spiritual overtones. Rumors circulated that some of the artists were somehow in league with the devil. Dark gothic overtones and cryptic, curious lyrics all helped fuel the narrative. Satanic High Priest Anton LaVey supposedly was the inspiration for the Eagles hit, "Hotel California." Occultist Aleister Crowley managed to influence many in the 60s, even though he was dead. Bands like Led Zeppelin, Black Sabbath, and Alice

Cooper made the occult and the devil very popular. Makeup artists even did some musicians up in provocative, supposedly-evil garb. Publicists made sure there was a steady flow of outlandish rumors to fill the gossip rags at grocery store checkout lines.

Though many people saw the hoopla as PR gimmicks to sell products, after all these years, it seems to me that many of these artists and their lyrics have been used by the devil to show his hand. In 1968, the first song on the Rolling Stones album *Beggar's Banquet* was a song called, "Sympathy for the Devil."

In that song, Mick Jagger sings from the perspective of the devil. He takes credit for various human evils in history, and then demands sympathy and respect from human beings. In fact, in one line, he even demands "politeness" from human beings, before threatening that he will "lay your soul to waste." Out of the other side of his mouth, he claims that the listener is to blame for these human evils, that "every cop is a criminal," and that all the sinners are "saints." In one of the most telling lines, the "devil" says that he watched in glee while human beings killed each other "for the gods they made."

Another song that came to my mind was written just two years after "Sympathy for the Devil" in 1970. It's a song called "Woodstock" by Joni Mitchell. Mitchell's lyrics show the softer side of Satanic deception, the hippie peace-love notion that we must fix the woes of the planet through the realization of our higher selves.

In the song, Mitchell explains that she came upon a "child of God" who was on a mission to set his own soul free. But this determined child of God doesn't stop there. Recognizing that he is only "billion-year-old-carbon" and "stardust" and that we are currently living in "the time of man," our supposedly-noble friend concludes that we—meaning humanity—must "get ourselves back to the garden."

Note the themes of the two songs. In one the devil is demanding respect for his behind-the-scenes mayhem and orchestration of history. He got his sympathy and homage from generations who fashioned gods of their own preferences and then slaughtered those who opposed them. In the other, he seduces humanity by mischaracterizing the God of the Bible—who has apparently abandoned us—promising peace and love in exchange for earth worship and doctrines of demons.

Throughout human history, the devil has sold the same lies to humankind over and over and over—and somehow we keep falling for it.

WHO IS THE REAL ENEMY?

Music, politics, and culture are inextricably bound together. "Politics is downstream from culture," one reporter said. One of the most powerful figures in modern politics was the late Saul Alinsky, who wrote a book that has become, for all intents and purposes, the American version of Mao's little red book. Alinsky titled it *Rules for Radicals*. Major political figures, presidents, and presidential wannabes have been followers of Alinsky. Hillary Clinton cited him as the inspiration for her master's thesis, which she titled, "There Is Only the Fight: An Analysis of the Alinsky Model."

Having read Alinsky's book several times, I was primarily

struck by what he wrote in the acknowledgment section of his book[2]:

"Lest we forget at least an over-the-shoulder acknowledgment to the very first radical: from all our legends, mythology, and history (and who is to know where mythology leaves off and history begins — or which is which), the first radical known to man who rebelled against the establishment and did it so effectively that he at least won his own kingdom — Lucifer."

— SAUL ALINSKY, *RULES FOR RADICALS*

Some infer that Alinsky was just being Alinsky, provoking a response. Fact-checkers rush to his defense saying his remark was tongue in cheek. However, Paul Kengor of *Crisis Magazine* adds some important context, when he writes, "Such a take on Lucifer isn't entirely unusual among socialists. In fact, Alinsky's angle on Lucifer is very similar to Mikhail Bakunin's in his own 1871 magnum opus, *God and the State*, which lauded Lucifer as 'the eternal rebel, the first freethinker.' To avoid overstatement and hyperbole, we should clarify that it would not be quite accurate to say that *Rules for Radicals* is 'dedicated' to Lucifer, as is often claimed by Alinsky's detractors. Regardless, that acknowledgment, or epigraph, is there, and it certainly tells us something."[3]

For anyone who's not convinced by Alinsky's plain statement in the epigraph of his own book, Kengor points to further proof of exactly where Alinsky stood on the issue of Satan. Alinsky was interviewed for the March 1972 issue of

Playboy magazine. In that interview, Alinsky was asked for his thoughts on the afterlife.

PLAYBOY: Having accepted your own mortality, do you believe in any kind of afterlife?

ALINSKY: Sometimes it seems to me that the question people should ask is not "Is there life after death?" but "Is there life after birth?" I don't know whether there's anything after this or not. I haven't seen the evidence one way or the other and I don't think anybody else has either. But I do know that man's obsession with the question comes out of his stubborn refusal to face up to his own mortality. Let's say that if there is an afterlife, and I have anything to say about it, I will unreservedly choose to go to hell.

PLAYBOY: Why?

ALINSKY: Hell would be heaven for me. All my life I've been with the have-nots. Over here, if you're a have-not, you're short of dough. If you're a have-not in hell, you're short of virtue. Once I get into hell, I'll start organizing the have-nots over there.

PLAYBOY: Why them?

ALINSKY: They're my kind of people.

When we consider Lucifer and his influence in history, at the very least, we have two diametrically opposed world views. In the biblical account, the affairs of man are viewed in the context of a holy God, a battle with an angelic rebel, and a coming cataclysmic event that will settle things forever. In the other view, man is seen as the captain of his own soul. It is a matter of the aggrieved rebelling against the oppressors and then bringing about a revolution that will result in some sort of utopia.

In yet another hallmark of Satan himself, Alinsky taught his followers to mask their agenda. But make no mistake; those like Alinsky often show their hands, if one looks closely enough.

"They have the guns and therefore we are for peace and for reformation through the ballot. **When we have the guns then it will be through the bullet**."

— SAUL ALINSKY, *RULES FOR RADICALS*

The enemy is often "hidden in plain sight."

So, who is the enemy?

There was a comic strip years ago called "Pogo" by Walt Kelly. In one particular episode, Pogo announces, **"We have met the enemy and he is us."**[4]

Numerous times in the Old Testament, God would ask, "Son of man what do you see?" The prophet would answer. Then the Lord would reveal what He was about to do. One day, as I stood in the Pile watching them sift for severed limbs while the heap of rubble belched out its toxic fumes, I imagined the Lord asking me, "Son of man, what do you see?"

My response was, "I see destruction—broken things, broken people, a broken nation—a broken world."

SON OF MAN, WHAT DO YOU SEE?

If the Lord were to ask me today, "Son of man, what do you see?" I would have to respond, "A world that is rejecting You, Lord. A world that clings to pagan notions about the earth, practices the worship of false gods, and is deceived and blinded by Satan, and by their own sin."

It is not for us to know precisely where we are in God's plan. In every crisis, there are faux prophets and pseudo-authorities who wax eloquent about "what is really going on." Rarely if ever are these people humble enough to admit they are wrong, or at the very least, that they don't know *for sure* what they are talking about. Instead, they are prophesying out of their own imagination or worse, their own desires.

After receiving astonishing revelations from God about things pertaining to future events, Daniel wrote:

> The man clothed in linen, who was above the waters of the river, lifted his right hand and his left hand toward heaven, and I heard him swear by him who lives forever, saying, "It will be for a time, times and half a time. When the power of the holy people has been finally broken, all these things will be completed."

> I heard, but I did not understand. So I asked, "My lord, what will the outcome of all this be?"

> He replied, "Go your way, Daniel, because the words are rolled up and sealed until the time of the end. Many will be purified, made spotless and refined, but the wicked will continue to be wicked. None of the wicked will understand,

but those who are wise will understand . . . As for you, go your way till the end.

— DANIEL 12:7-10, 13 NIV

Jesus told us plainly in the book of Acts, "It is not for you to know the times or dates the Father has set . . . but you will receive power when the Holy Spirit comes on you."

One of our biggest enemies, and maybe even our biggest, is our own sinful nature. Whether it is a mullah or a molecule that causes someone to reject the one true God, the dire straits we find ourselves in are a direct result of turning our backs to God instead of our faces. This is the judgment we are experiencing—not that one country takes over another or another dictator wreaks havoc and commits genocide—no, "this is the judgment that the Light has come into the world, but men preferred the darkness because their deeds were evil."

We don't need a paradigm shift or a new deal or a revolution—we need a Savior.

Jesus promises to return for those who long for His appearing. The next time He comes, though, it will not be as a baby, peacefully lying in a manger. The next time, He will be leading the armies of Heaven.

I saw heaven standing open and there before me was a white horse, whose rider is called Faithful and True. With justice he judges and wages war. His eyes are like blazing fire, and on his head are many crowns. He has a name written on him that no one knows but he himself. He is dressed in a robe dipped in blood, and his name is the Word of God. The armies of heaven were following him, riding on white horses and dressed in fine linen, white and clean. Coming out of his mouth is a sharp sword with which to strike down the nations. "He will rule them with an iron scepter." He treads the winepress of the fury of the wrath of God Almighty. On his robe and on his thigh he has this name written:

KING OF KINGS AND LORD OF LORDS.

— REVELATION 19:11-16

NIV

Lord, we face an uncertain future, and it appears that great storms are on the horizon. So we pray in agreement with your Word. Search us, Oh Lord.

Not politicians. Not political parties. Not nations. Not news outlets.

Search me, Oh God, and know my heart.

Try me, and know my anxious thoughts.

And see if there is any wicked way in me.

And lead me in the way everlasting.

13

RESHAPED FOR A PURPOSE

THE AMOUNT of rubble removed from Ground Zero was staggering. What did they do with it after their investigations were concluded? Where did it all go? Was any of it usable?

A 2016 PBS NewsHour program reported on what became of the remnants of the World Trade Center. According to an article written by Michael D. Regan, the Port Authority of New York and New Jersey was responsible for handling some 2600 artifacts collected from the site in Hangar 17 at John F. Kennedy International Airport.

The Port Authority created a program which oversaw the distribution of Ground Zero items to 1585 fire departments, museums, municipalities, and other organizations, so that they could commemorate heroes and memorialize those who lost their lives.[1]

Using those artifacts, many monuments, displays, and memorials were created. Perhaps among the most intriguing —a Navy ship.

THE USS NEW YORK

On November 7th, 2009, the United States Navy officially commissioned the *USS New York*. The ship was named at the request then Governor George Pataki, who wanted to honor the victims of 9/11. During construction, 7.5 tons of World Trade Center steel were used on the *USS New York*.

The ship's motto is "Never Forget" and reminders of 9/11 are found throughout the ship in various displays and memorials. The chaplain of the ship even chooses one victim's name to honor each day during his daily prayer service.

As a Navy Chaplain, I have had the privilege to offer invocations at many types of ceremonies. One favorite memory was praying at the commissioning ceremony for a new Coast Guard Icebreaker. I remember that my prayer reflected the nature of her mission—cutting through the ice to open the sea lanes for other ships.

The keel of a ship is the bottom-middle foundation of a ship, and is special for several reasons. First, an event known as "laying the keel" marks the official start of a ship's construction—a practice which dates back to ancient times. In fact, there are still traditions in place today that date back to ancient Greece, such as laying a newly minted coin under the keel. This tradition is believed to have originated with the belief about having to pay a ferryman to transport souls across the river Styx, in case the ship were to sink.

The bow of a large steel ship is the part out in front. It is basically the forward most part of the keel. As part of the bow, the WTC steel will always be the first part of the ship to sail into the future, 21st-century expeditionary warfare missions.

There is significance to the bow of the *USS New York* being the section of ship created with World Trade Center steel. The bow is the part of the ship that cuts through the waves, and in concert with the keel, helps in counterbalancing the winds. What was once destroyed is now being used to protect, defend, and keep peace.

Tony Quaglino, a crane superintendent who worked on construction of the *USS New York*, described his experience. "Most all of us considered the bow stem containing the WTC steel very special. Many of us working on the ship, including myself, felt a need to touch it and try to experience and understand the grief of those who died and the loss of all who loved them and had to go on," he continued. "It was then and is still now our only way to personally connect to the tragic events of 9/11. I felt that in many ways this was as brutal and devastating an attack on our nation as was Pearl Harbor, when I was a child."[2]

As I thought about the *USS New York* being constructed, I began to reflect on the imagery of the dry dock, and how existing vessels are taken into dry docks for decommissioning, refitting, and recommissioning. Take for instance the two USNS hospital ships, the *USNS Comfort* and the *USNS Mercy*.

I've already shared the powerful effect the arrival of the *Comfort* had on me personally at Ground Zero. But the *Mercy* also has a stellar record of inspirational service—touching lives, saving lives, bringing healing. Looking into the history of these ships, I learned that both of them were formerly oilers —a U.S. Navy ship used to refuel other ships and restock them with food, ammunition, and other necessities. At some point, both the *Mercy* and the *Comfort* were refitted to suit their new missions.

BEING REFIT FOR THE MASTER'S USE

On this twentieth anniversary of 9/11, as we face an uncertain future and a season of global unrest, my mind goes to language from the Bible that refers to you and me as vessels. Paul, when writing to the Romans, reminds them that the Lord has purposes that are all His own—they're not the same as our purpose. He, as the potter, can do whatever He chooses with the vessels He has made.

> But who are you, a human being, to talk back to God? "Shall what is formed say to the one who formed it, 'Why did you make me like this?'" Does not the potter have the right to make out of the same lump of clay some pottery for special purposes and some for common use?

> What if God, although choosing to show his wrath and make his power known, bore with great patience the objects of his wrath—prepared for destruction? What if he did this to make the riches of his glory known to the objects of his mercy, whom he prepared in advance for glory.

> — ROMANS 9:20-23 NIV

The vessel itself doesn't matter as much as what the vessel contains. The same steel that makes an oil tanker can be refitted to carry troops to and from war. It can carry arms, anesthetics, cannons, or care packages for disaster

FROM RUBBLE TO REDEMPTION

relief. It all comes down to the plans of the Master Shipmaker.

Whether you and I are fashioned to cut through the icy fear that has frozen us in place, fitted for conflict, or in a season of dry dock, waiting for orders—it's all up to God. How the Lord uses us, and into what seas He launches us, is not ours to choose. He gives the orders. We can, however, choose *how we respond* to His plans.

In the last letter he ever wrote, Paul told Timothy that you and I are vessels to be used by the Master however He wishes:

> Nevertheless the solid foundation of God stands, having this seal: "The Lord knows those who are His," and, "Let everyone who names the name of Christ depart from iniquity."

> But in a great house there are not only vessels of gold and silver, but also of wood and clay, some for honor and some for dishonor. Therefore if anyone cleanses himself from the latter, he will be a vessel for honor, sanctified and useful for the Master, prepared for every good work.

> — 2 TIMOTHY 2:19-21 NKJV

It is not for us to explain everything that befalls us. However, it is our responsibility to act on what we know to be revealed in God's Word. Judgment is a subject we would prefer not to discuss in this era of postmodern ambiguity. *Who am I to judge?* we like to ask. Sounds noble, but it can also reflect a desire to avoid certain aspects of God's truth.

Jesus said in John 12:47, "For I did not come to judge the

world, but to save the world." But immediately after that, in the very next verse of the Bible, He reminds us of the uncomfortable truth. "There is a judge for the one who rejects me and does not accept my words; the very words I have spoken will condemn them at the last day" (John 12:48 NIV).

God loved the world on 9/11, and He still loves the world. Men loved the darkness—the shadiness of their own desires. They still do.

But the Master? His plans are not up for debate. This world belongs to Him, and everything in it. He has the final say, so we would be wise to surrender ourselves to Him, and cooperate with His plans. When we do that, we will be able to withstand anything this world throws at us, and we will go safely with Him into eternity.

Build me straight, O worthy Master!
Stanch and strong, a goodly vessel,
That shall laugh at all disaster,
And with wave and whirlwind wrestle.

— HENRY WADSWORTH
LONGFELLOW, *THE BUILDING OF*
THE SHIP

Dear Lord, Make me a vessel unto honor. Help me wrestle with the waves and the whirlwinds, confident of this one thing: No purposes of yours can be thwarted and your promises are fixed and true. Fix my course to the Morning Star, and see me safely home.

UNDER THE COVERS

MY PARENTS WERE AMAZING PEOPLE, but I didn't always appreciate that. They were both extremely intelligent. Neither one was afforded the luxury of going to college. They raised five children, each of which possessed a deep conviction that we live to serve others and to obey God. My parents fought hard against the odds. They endured. They persevered.

Looking back, I have come to realize that the Great Depression, as it came to be known, had a profound effect on each of them in different ways. I remember my mom saving almost everything—even empty food jars and Ziploc bags. My dad spent his entire career at the same desk faithfully providing for his family, all the while battling personal demons and enduring chronic pain.

I can remember the smell of incense wafting through St. Columba Cathedral, where the Jenkins boys could always be counted on to serve at the altar after being dispatched in our starched white shirts to walk there in the dark at 6 a.m. Mom and Dad saw to it that we were always in church.

Every Christmas our family would give the priest some special gift. The nuns would get handpicked lotions from Woolworths. The church was an integral part of our lives. I had a sense of awe when it came to God, but truth be known, I also came away with a deeply ingrained notion that I had to make up for everything I did wrong. I felt that I had to examine my own conscience to accuse myself before God. The notion that I somehow had to earn my way back into God's good graces created a mindset that affected how I saw God. Whether it was intended or not, I always came away with the belief that I had to clean up my act before I was worthy to receive communion—and that if I were to die in a state of unworthiness, I would be lost forever.

Youngstown, Ohio, offered limited opportunities. Growing up in a steel town that was dying (we just didn't know it yet), the ticket out was usually some kind of achievement. For example, an athletic scholarship was usually deemed as a sure road to success. Another way out might be a congressional appointment to a military academy.

DREAMING

As a teenager, I began to fantasize about how I might have a successful life. For some reason, I was always fascinated with the Army-Navy football game. When the cadets would march into the stadium wearing those amazing uniforms, I made myself a promise: "One day I'm going to be like them." I fantasized that my dad and mom would be in the crowd at Annapolis when the graduation ceremonies were wrapping up. The newly commissioned officers would all throw our caps into the air. "That's our son," my parents would proudly boast.

As the steel mills began to close, and the world seemed to radically tilt on its axis, my parents began to suffer from the accumulated damage their bodies had received during their difficult lives. They had lived through the Great Depression, WWII, the Korean War, and now Vietnam.

But for young people in America, change was in the air. It was the summer of '69.

As my high school career was ending, it became painfully clear that I was not all-city material on the football field. By this point, my father had to wear a painful back brace. He had to walk with a cane or crutches. My mother pushed on, trying her best to "get the last one through high school" while my siblings all carved out their own journeys.

The Vietnam War was starting to hit close to home. JFK, Martin Luther King Jr., and Bobby Kennedy had all been assassinated. One year after my graduation, I was driving on the interstate, and I will always remember what happened. I passed the troop trucks carrying National Guardsmen on their way to Kent State University, which is about 45 miles west of Youngstown.

As graduation neared, I was anxious to get out there and make a name for myself. I wanted to show everybody that I was okay. Being partial to Navy uniforms, I began the application process for a congressional appointment to Annapolis. Somehow, I squeaked by and got the requisite SAT scores.

I'll never forget the day I got a letter from the congressman's office. It was a surreal experience. He had already used all of his appointments, but he did find a colleague from out west somewhere who had one appointment left. It was for the Merchant Marine Academy. I was going to be a cadet—just like the guys on TV! Looking back, two things stick out about this event. First, I don't remember either of my parents reacting or saying a word about me being appointed to a service academy. Second, I do remember that at the awards ceremony for the class of 1969, it was announced that Jim Jenkins was appointed to the Merchant Marine Academy.

Commencement took place in June, and I made the rounds to various graduation parties. It began to dawn on me that I had signed onto a career that I knew nothing about. Scheduled to depart for Long Island, New York, in July, it hit me that I was going to move away from home for the first time. Anxious thoughts began to plague my mind. I did my best to suppress them.

A week or so before I was to leave for Long Island, my dad got up out of bed and his hip broke. He was suffering from a debilitating case of osteoporosis, and his brittle bones just gave way. The ambulance came to take him to the hospital. I remember the look on my mom's face. In a very short time, he developed a pulmonary embolism and the next thing I remember was my mom putting a rosary in his hand while the rest of us prayed. He lay there dying at the age of 54.

Something shut down inside of me.

THE BROKEN PIECES

Through the years when I have looked back on this event, I have been unable to ascertain exactly how I got to the academy. But as best I can recall, I left very shortly after the funeral and traveled to Kings Point, New York, which is on the furthest point of the tip of Long Island. I was now a cadet at the United States Merchant Marine Academy.

Plebe (the academy word for "freshman") summers are notorious. I was aware that it was going to be extremely stressful by design. I'm not sure if it was the trauma of my father's passing, but not only do I not remember exactly how I got there, I don't remember any of the check-in procedures. No details about those first few days. All I remember is that I had not shut my eyes for over 48 hours.

Then the worst possible thing happened, at least from my perspective: Neil Armstrong set foot on the moon. Because of the momentous nature of the moon landing, all federal employees deemed non-essential had the day off. This meant that our training schedule was suspended. We were allowed to sit by ourselves in our rooms. But the last thing I needed was time to sit and think.

As I looked up at the moon that night something started to give way inside me. A guy was walking on the moon! And we just buried my dad. I was exhausted, but couldn't sleep. I went out into the hall to find the bathroom. An upperclassman spotted me. Walking briskly up to me, he got right in my face and told me to brace; stand at rigid attention—suck in my chin —stare straight ahead and wait for what was coming next. That's all I remember.

When I came to, I was completely disoriented. I had no idea where I was or how I got there, but I could tell that I was in a hospital bed. I looked to my right and saw a young man with what appeared to be a recent amputation of his leg. I looked to my left and saw another young man with a horrible wound on his face. Then the trembling started. I shook so bad that I felt the bed move. I pulled the covers up over my head and for the first time in my life—I prayed.

I was a religious person. Quite often, I *recited* lots of different prayers. For my whole life, as far back as I can remember, I *read* aloud many prayers in liturgical settings. But this time was different. This time, I genuinely talked to God.

"Dear God, I'm scared right now. I don't know what's happening to me and I feel like I'm losing my grip. Help me! Show me the way!"

My memory is spotty as to what happened next. All I know is that I fell asleep. I don't know how long I slept, but I when I woke up, I learned that I was in a public service hospital in New York City. I had collapsed at the academy and they had brought me to the hospital. Two Merchant Marine officers were standing at the foot of my bed. To this day I don't know if one of them was a chaplain, but I assume he must have been.

They explained that I had collapsed and that the diagnosis was an acute anxiety reaction due to the sudden death of my father and the rigors of the first few days of Plebe summer with no sleep. They informed me of a choice that now lay before me. "You have two options. You are already behind. You can attempt to rejoin your class and get up to speed or, due to the unique circumstances, you can resign your appointment and return home—no harm, no foul."

I couldn't even think straight, and I was so weak that I couldn't even imagine jumping into the discipline of a Plebe summer. Adding to that was the fact that deep down, I had done all of this to please my father. But now he was gone.

I chose to return home.

I enrolled in Youngstown State University, got a job as an orderly at a mental hospital, and started trying to put one foot in front of the other. I kept a low profile and began working full-time while also taking a full load at school. The remainder of the time I spent in the pubs with my friends. I didn't let myself think very much about my failure, or the incredible opportunity I had wasted with the academy appointment. I just tried to do what everyone else was doing in the late '60s.

A couple of years passed and one day I got a call from my brother-in-law. He invited me to attend a meeting of the Holy Name Society, a men's group at the Catholic church. "Don't let the name put you off," he explained, "We tap a keg and watch Notre Dame football movies. I want you to join so you can vote for me to be the president. It will be great for my insurance business." He wasn't kidding about any of it.

As it turns out, they did have beer at the very first meeting I attended, but this meeting was going to be different. The priest introduced a chubby little man with an infectious grin. He was a protestant minister who was going to give his 'testimony'—whatever that meant. As this pastor began to tell his story about how he had been "born again," I began to get physically uncomfortable. I had never heard language like that in my life. I wanted to run out of the building.

It was not that I disbelieved what he was saying about the possibility of having a personal relationship with God. In fact, deep down, I knew he was telling the truth! But something about his testimony made me uncomfortable. Still, I managed to stay till the end.

After the meeting, a young guy came up to me and asked,

"You're Jim Jenkins, aren't you? You don't remember me, do you?"

This guy had the same clear-eyed joy I had noticed in the minister. The guy told me his name, and I remembered the last time I saw him. It was in high school. This guy was so totally transformed that I had not recognized him. We talked for a minute, then he invited me to go and hear this minister again at his church on the coming Sunday night. Just to get rid of him, I agreed to go. Driving away that night I thought, "What have I gotten myself into?"

I wasn't prepared for what I saw that Sunday night. This small church out in the middle of nowhere was completely packed. People were standing in the foyer, sitting on the carpet at the front, and many more were outside waiting to get into the church! The music was unlike anything I had ever heard in church. I spotted my high school algebra teacher—a nun wearing her habit—next to a menacing-looking Hell's Angel biker in his leathers. Both were lifting their hands and praising God. I was excited by what I saw and felt, but I still tried my best to let everyone know that I was only visiting. Every Sunday night for about a month, I came back to this little church.

During that same time period, a buddy of mine told me, "Man you need to quit working at that mental hospital. It's affecting you and that's all you ever talk about." He was right. Things were intense at work. So much was changing. I resigned, assuming I could pick up another job pretty easily. But it didn't happen nearly as fast as I had imagined. Because I was out of work, I missed two car payments. Then I was told that my car would be repossessed if I didn't make a payment of $104.00.

I redoubled my effort to find work. The last place I tried was a rehab facility that specialized in treating spinal cord injuries. The HR lady told me, "Look, I'll be honest with you. We don't have any openings and frankly don't anticipate any. I'll keep your resume but there are at least three men ahead of you on a waiting list." To top things off, I was more than a little depressed that I hadn't seen any of the guys I worked with at the mental hospital. We were close, and I hadn't heard from any of them in weeks.

SOMETHING REAL

One Sunday night, there were hundreds of people crammed into the little church. But as the preacher gave his message, it felt like I was the only person in the room. He said, "Are you tired of trying to manage your life and deal with your failures and sins on your own? It's not up to you to pay for your sins and to make up for your failures. You can give all the broken pieces of your life tonight to a God who loves you so much that he sent His Son, Jesus, to die in your place. You can be born again, right now."

I went to the front and dropped to my knees. Confessing that I was a sinner, I made a decision—I wanted what Jesus did on the cross to count for me.

It was as if a large boil had been lanced, and all the pus of bitterness and shame came oozing out. I wept and I laughed. I knew that I knew that I knew—that something real had just transpired. I knew that God had answered the prayer I uttered under the covers in that public service hospital in New York. God was real, and He was about to show me the way.

The next day, I had to drop off a term paper near the quad

on campus. I heard a familiar voice yelling, "Jenkins, wait up!" It was one of my orderly buddies from the mental hospital. "Man, I've been trying to get a hold of you. I lost your phone number. All the guys are asking about you." I was very glad to learn that they hadn't forgotten me. I remember being greatly moved to know that these guys were still my friends. But true to my cautious nature, I was hesitant to link this with what happened the night before.

After that, I drove home so I could be there when the repo man came to take my car. For some reason, I wasn't bothered at all. I was sitting near the front porch waiting for him to come and take my car, and yet I had this strange peace.

I heard the mailman closing our mailbox and saw a letter addressed to me from the University Bursar's Office. I didn't even know what a bursar was, but I assumed that now I was going to owe them money as well. I opened the letter:

Dear Mr. Jenkins,

*Our records indicate that two semesters ago, an error occurred when processing your account. Please find enclosed our check **in the amount of $104.00.** (emphasis added)*

It was the exact amount I needed to stop my car from getting repossessed—to the penny. While I was still holding the letter in my trembling hand, the phone rang.

"May I speak with James Jenkins?"

"This is James Jenkins."

FROM RUBBLE TO REDEMPTION

"Hi, James. Hillside Hospital human resources calling. A very strange thing happened this morning. All three men ahead of you on our waiting list called in one after another and informed us that they had taken other jobs. We have an opening. Can you start next week?"

I knelt down and praised God.

I have doubted myself many times over the years. I have been used mightily by the Lord, and I have also miserably failed Him on many occasions. Yet I can never deny that He revealed Himself to me and has led me to a life of adventure I could have never imagined.

Forty years of public ministry.

Twenty-one of those years as a military chaplain.

Decades of teaching seminary students.

A family so wonderful, I know I don't deserve them.

But most of all, the absolute surety of eternal life based on what Jesus did for me on the cross.

This book is about how the Lord can reach us, even at the Pile. Even when we are buried in the rubble and the debris of our own sinfulness, God finds us and saves us. But He also uses the wreckage and the wasted places of our lives for His purposes.

GOD'S FINGERPRINTS

Years after 9/11, I was giving my testimony at an anniversary observance. I told the people gathered there that I had only been to New York City twice—once when my nephew was married, and then again in 2001. As soon as I said it, I felt something. I couldn't put my finger on it—something wasn't right. Later that night it came to me. Like pieces of a jigsaw puzzle, it all came together. I remembered something that I had all but forgotten.

During my time serving at Ground Zero, our Chaplains Emergency Response Team was billeted at a Coast Guard facility on Staten Island. It was from that place that we traveled daily to the Pile. It was to that place we returned to reflect on what happened that day, to debrief, and to pray for one another. Could it be? Where did they take me in July of 1969? I know I was in New York City, but where in New York City?

I got out my computer and looked up a map of Staten Island. Then I Googled "Public Service Hospital and Staten Island." Bingo! The place where I prayed with the covers over my head in 1969, as Neil Armstrong walked on the Moon, was just a few miles away from the site known as Fresh Kills! During my time at Ground Zero, I had billeted just a few miles from where the public service hospital was located. I have since learned that the place was called Bayley Seton Hospital, and it was the location of one of the greatest failures of my life.

After 9/11 happened, the Lord brought me back to the place of my failure and put me smack-dab in the middle of the worst debris field in American history. This time I did not come as a cocky cadet, but as a humbled chaplain. In 1969, I washed out.

But now, 32 years later, I returned—washed in the blood of the Lamb, and ready to serve His purposes. I was privileged to come in the Name of the Lord to the rubble and the death and the ruins—to the siege mounds of the Pile and Fresh Kills—with living proof that there is a loving God who cares enough to be with us at every turn.

Twenty years later the siege goes on. Plagues, global unrest, and great uncertainty are affecting us all. An enemy has done this.

And yet none of it has escaped the notice of our God. Jesus Christ is the same yesterday, today, and forever.

May I invite you to do something? Each of us has a personal pile. Our landscape is littered with the debris of heartaches, losses, and failures. Why not find a spot in your debris field, clear a place amidst the rubble of your fears and failures, pull the covers up over your face with your trembling hands, and call out to God?

He's been waiting for you.

15

THE STRUGGLE TO EXPLAIN HUMAN SUFFERING

And we know that in all things God works for the good of
those who love him, who have been called according to his
purpose.

— ROMANS 8:28 NIV

"THE PATIENCE OF JOB" has become a proverb and an adage.
It is used to describe human resilience and endurance in the
face of adversity, or longsuffering through times of great loss.
In the book of the Bible that bears his name, we read:

Then the LORD said to Satan, "Have you considered my
servant Job? There is no one on earth like him; he is
blameless and upright, a man who fears God and shuns
evil. And he still maintains his integrity, though you incited
me against him to ruin him without any reason." . . .

So Satan went out from the presence of the LORD and afflicted Job with painful sores from the soles of his feet to the crown of his head. Then Job took a piece of broken pottery and scraped himself with it as he sat among the ashes . . .

In all this, Job did not sin in what he said.

— JOB 2:3, 7-8, 10 NIV

Another saying that has worked its way into our language is the phrase "Job's comforters." This has come to describe people who offer trite or hurtful remarks about those who are enduring terrible suffering.

Job's friends actually started out doing the right thing. Just like Job had done, they tore their robes and put dust on their heads. In ancient times, these were signs of mourning or repentance, or both. So Job's friends just sat with him for the first seven days after their arrival, mourning alongside Job without saying a word. But then they began to speak, and from that point on, the majority of the book involves Job's friends accusing him of wrongdoing.

Job responds in chapter 16 by telling them that he's heard all of their accusations and reasonings many times over, and then he proclaims, "You are miserable comforters, all of you!"

DOES A "REASON" EVEN EXIST?

While the humans around Job did not handle his situation very well, what's usually more perplexing for readers are the questions about God, the devil, and their respective roles in

Job's suffering. What was the point of God allowing his servant to endure such a cataclysmic loss? Was it Satan's idea to incite God to test Job so sorely? Or was it God's idea? What role did Job have—was it Job's sinfulness, or his children's recklessness? Was it his fear that opened a door for the enemy? He says in Job 3:25, "For the thing I greatly feared has come upon me, and what I dreaded has happened to me."

We only have speculations. Guesses. The Bible never gives us a clear reason for Job's suffering. We see little glimpses of how the whole thing played out in Heaven and on earth, but we don't ever really get the "reason." Is there a clear reason that we would understand? We simply don't know if that reason exists, much less what it is.

I will probably always remember a remark I heard at a pastors' conference years ago. The presenter said, "Maybe all we can say for certain is that Job was allowed to go through what he did simply so he could write a book about it to help us when we suffer inexplicable tragedies."

Inexplicable.

SOMETIMES THERE IS A REASON

For I do not want you to be ignorant of the fact, brothers and sisters, that our ancestors were all under the cloud and that they all passed through the sea. They were all baptized into Moses in the cloud and in the sea. They all ate the same spiritual food and drank the same spiritual drink; for they drank from the spiritual rock that accompanied them, and that rock was Christ. Nevertheless, God was not pleased with most of them; their bodies were scattered in the wilderness.

Now these things occurred as examples to keep us from setting our hearts on evil things as they did.

— 1 CORINTHIANS 10:1-6 NIV

According to the Bible, when human beings set their hearts on evil, bad things can happen as a result.

Am I inferring that the Pile in New York was proof of God's judgment on the individuals who perished? No.

Am I even saying that America was to blame? No.

What I am saying is that when you have suffered enormous loss and you sit with your robe torn, scraping yourself with debris, and sprinkling dust on your head—you have come face to face, like it or not, with some hard questions.

Who is God?

What is He like?

Is there more to life than this?

Are there truly—like my mortician friend at the Morgue said—far worse things than dying?

The traditions of tearing one's clothes, shaving one's head, and throwing dust on one's head—all speak to the reality that we are creatures. The word "creatures" carries with it the identity of created beings. We are not self-made, nor are we self-sustaining. We don't answer only to ourselves. There is a higher authority.

And we are all in constant need of repentance for ignoring

the God who made us. How many times have we heard it recited at a gravesite?

"Ashes to ashes. Dust to dust."

That ritual of pouring dust on one's head may signify to us that *we can* begin to "get our heads around" the unthinkable— once we humble ourselves, acknowledge our true condition, and bow in worship. About a third of the way through the book of Job, we read that Job declared: "Though He slay me, yet will I trust Him" (Job 13:15).

The Pile was awful and there were no words to adequately comfort. Still, the fact remains that God revealed Himself in the rubble. As Job sat in the ash heap while his friends kept trying to convince him that he must have done something wrong, Job got painfully honest with them. I remember visiting a man from my congregation who was dying from pancreatic cancer. It was painful and frightening. One day as I watched him suffer, he groaned. I leaned in close, and said, "I know . . . I know . . . " He opened his eyes, reached up, grabbed my shirt, yanked me in close, and said, "No! You don't know!"

Job's friends didn't understand his pain either. He repeatedly put his grievances to words, while fully accepting the fact that they would not be understood by the people around him. At one point, out of extreme frustration, he implores his "comforters" to have mercy:

> "Have pity on me, my friends, have pity,
>   for the hand of God has struck me.
> Why do you pursue me as God does?
>   Will you never get enough of my flesh?
> "Oh, that my words were recorded,

that they were written on a scroll,
that they were inscribed with an iron
  tool on lead,
or engraved in rock forever!
I know that my redeemer lives,
  and that in the end he will stand on the earth.
And after my skin has been destroyed,
  yet in my flesh I will see God;
I myself will see him
  with my own eyes—I, and not another.
How my heart yearns within me!

— JOB 19:21-27 NIV

As it turned out, his words were recorded. And it also worked out for Job that in his earthly life, God was not done with him. The book of Job ends with Job realizing that God is sovereign—He is not required to answer to human questioning, complaints, or judgment. He does not have to explain His reasons to us. This is something we can all observe directly to be true in our own lives. God can give us an explanation if He wants to, but He certainly doesn't have to.

As the passage in 1 Corinthians makes clear, sometimes there is a reason why terrible things happen. But that doesn't mean we will necessarily get a clear answer to our question when we search for one. Still, we will almost always get a response.

When Job was finished with his complaint, God spoke to him out of the storm, basically letting Job know that He did not have to answer to Him. Job seems to have come into agreement with that truth. His humble reply to God was, "Surely I spoke of things I did not understand, things too wonderful for me to know . . . Therefore, I despise myself and repent in dust and ashes" (Job 42:3, 6).

The Bible goes on to record that the Lord blessed the latter part of Job's life even more than He had in the previous part. The Apostle James tells us that the prophets of the Lord are an example for us of patience in the face of suffering. Then he mentions Job, and how God finally brought about good again in Job's life, before adding, "The Lord is full of compassion and mercy."

Full.

BEAUTY FOR ASHES

I have only a few mementos of my time at the Pile. One is my ID badge. The other is the pair of boots that I wore. I always remember two things when I see the boots. First, I was so preoccupied and anxious about traveling to New York that I packed two different boots from two separate pairs. I didn't even realize I had done that until months after my return to Oregon.

Second, I have never cleaned them. They still have dust from Ground Zero on them. Every time I see them, I am reminded that God was in the Pile, and that I know that my Redeemer lives.

Years ago, when I was first saved, we used to sing a song that seems very fitting right now. The song lyrics were simply a portion of Scripture from Isaiah that had been set to music. This portion of Scripture is highly significant. When Jesus first began His earthly ministry, he stood up in the synagogue and read from this passage, and then declared that it had been fulfilled in their midst.

In other words, He was proclaiming that He had come into the world to do the things listed in that Scripture:

> The Spirit of the Sovereign LORD is on me,
>> because the LORD has anointed me
>> to proclaim good news to the poor.
> He has sent me to bind up the brokenhearted,
>> to proclaim freedom for the captives
>> and release from darkness for the prisoners,
> to proclaim the year of the LORD's favor
>> and the day of vengeance of our God,
> to comfort all who mourn,
>> and provide for those who grieve in Zion—
> **to bestow on them a crown of beauty**
>> **instead of ashes,**
> **the oil of joy**
>> **instead of mourning,**
> **and a garment of praise**
>> **instead of a spirit of despair.**
> They will be called oaks of righteousness,
>> a planting of the Lord
>> for the display of his splendor.
>
> — ISAIAH 61:1-3 NIV

Whenever life brings tragedy, just like Job, we must go through a process of grief. Mourning. Questioning. But in the end, Job's story shows us that the way to move forward is to recognize that we aren't God, and that He doesn't have to

FROM RUBBLE TO REDEMPTION

answer to us. We need Him. He does not need us. We are dependent on Him. He is not dependent on us. We come into agreement with this truth, and we will see good coming back into our lives.

What good could possibly come from the Pile? The Pile itself was not good. 9/11 was not good. There's nothing good about the terrorist attack, the towers falling, or people dying. But wherever there are ashes, Jesus Christ has the power to bring beauty out of them. Isaiah prophesied that the Lord would comfort and plant people as "oaks of righteousness." But in the next verse, he adds, "They will rebuild the ancient ruins and restore the places long devastated" (Isaiah 61:4 NIV). We have a part to play in His process of healing and restoration.

Beauty for ashes.

Praise instead of despair.

From out of the Pile, to the promise of eternal life.

From a broken world, to one made completely new.

The decision belongs to each individual.

THE FACE OF GOD

Now the Lord is the Spirit, and where the Spirit of the Lord is, there is freedom. And we all, who with unveiled faces contemplate the Lord's glory, are being transformed into his image with ever-increasing glory, which comes from the Lord, who is the Spirit.

— 2 CORINTHIANS 3:17-18 NIV

As BELIEVERS, we reflect the glory of the Lord. This can manifest in many ways as we encounter people throughout our lives. During my time at the Pile, the Lord used my face on three different occasions to show His presence and comfort to a hurting soul.

FIRST ENCOUNTER: MAYOR GIULIANI

The first time was on the very first ferry ride as we accompanied family members to see the Pile up close and personal. As I previously mentioned, Mayor Giuliani was on that first trip, and there was a divine moment that took place. On our return to the pier building where the Family Center was set up, he came over to me grabbed both my hands, and stared at my face. He had just seen the first family members' visit to the Pile, and he was fresh off the experience of one family member screaming at him and blaming him for the death of his son.

Mayor Giuliani was in the middle of trying to manage the biggest crisis of modern times. Yet for what seemed to be a very long time, he was staring at my face. It felt like something spiritual was being imparted to him. He said, "Thank you for coming here to help us." Our brief encounter was surreal, and this may sound strange, but when he said those words, I felt like he wasn't talking to me.

SECOND ENCOUNTER: ELTON JOHN

The next encounter came a few days later—again at the Family Center. There was so much going on at so many levels. Along with all the technical and logistical support of the families, there were also VIPs and celebrities coming by frequently to offer support. We were briefed on the protocol involved in case the Queen of Jordan happened to speak to us during her visit. Hall of Fame athletes like baseball's Mr. October, Reggie Jackson, movie stars, and rock stars were all doing their part to encourage and comfort family members.

One day, as I was talking to one of the family members at the Center, something was going on a few yards away. It was clear that someone very famous was being escorted through the area, and as he came into view, I could immediately recognize that it was Elton John. For some reason, I just blurted out, "Hey! Thanks for coming down here. I know you came down here to help."

He turned my way and began to walk toward me. As he walked toward me, he stared directly at my face. Then he came very close, cupped my face in his hands, and continued to stare intently. Again, I had this sense that it was not just my face he was seeing. After staring intently for several moments and then letting go of my face, Elton John turned and walked away from me without saying a word.

Twice, and maybe I could have chalked it up to a strange coincidence. But then it happened again.

THIRD ENCOUNTER: A GRIEVING FATHER

We were on another one of the trips escorting family members to the Pile. This one gentleman puzzled me. He was very distinguished looking, but that's not what was so perplexing. I knew that he would not have been on the boat unless he was a next of kin relative to someone who had perished. But his demeanor didn't fit. He seemed calm about everything— almost detached.

The man engaged me in conversation about what happened on that fateful day. I kept thinking that I had seen a lot of different grief reactions, but this was very different. When we finally got to the staging area and he saw the Pile, the blood drained out of his face and his knees buckled a bit. He began to cry, "My son. My son."

On the way back, this man poured out his heart to me. His son was one of the many tradesmen whose full-time job was maintaining the World Trade Center complex. After we prayed, he hugged me and thanked me—all while staring at my face.

Several days later, I heard through the grapevine that there was going to be a special service held at St Patrick's cathedral for all the tradespeople who had died on 9/11. I suggested to my boss that someone from our team of chaplains ought to be there. He and I both went.

We were seated at the very back. I was at the end of the aisle. The cathedral sanctuary has a capacity of three thousand people, and it was completely packed. As we sat there waiting for the service to begin, you could hear them coming. In the distance was the familiar rat-a-tat-tat of drums and the haunting sound of bagpipes getting ever clearer, closer, and louder. The cathedral's 20,000 pound bronze doors opened, and this magnificent sanctuary was filled with the overwhelming sound of the combined NYPD and FDNY pipe and drum corps.

The procession was led by someone carrying a cross, the Cardinal, and some other officiants. Huge banners were held by members of all the unions represented—plumbers, carpenters, and electricians. I will never forget the sights and sounds of that moment.

After they were all seated, the Cardinal began the Mass. It came time for communion. How on earth, I thought, are they going to serve communion to so many people? Incredibly and efficiently, they did just that.

We were so far back that the people at the front of the church looked tiny. I was watching the ushers move people along. Suddenly, there was a disruption at the front of the church. Someone appeared to be pushing past the ushers. We watched as a man pushed his way down the aisle and kept walking back.

All the way back to where we were.

It was then that I recognized who it was. It was the man from the ferry ride to Ground Zero. His eyes were filled with tears. He must have spotted me on the way in. He walked up to me, put his hands on my face, and said with earnest gratitude in his voice, "Thank you for coming. I knew you would come. I knew you would come."

Again, I don't know how to describe the experience other than to say that I'm pretty sure it wasn't me he was talking to. It felt like he was looking right past me even though he was looking directly into my face.

Am I saying that my face is like God's face? Of course not. Am I saying that there was something special about me? No, I am not saying that at all. I am saying that when we encounter someone—especially someone in crisis—and we are filled with God's Holy Spirit, our willingness to extend His grace and presence reveals His face to the person who is suffering.

GOD'S FAVOR

As I considered this whole notion of our faces reflecting the glory of God, I remembered the biblical story of Jacob and Esau. They were twins, and we read that at birth, Jacob was born literally grasping his older brother's heel. When they were grown and their father, Isaac, was ready to bestow the blessing on the firstborn son, Jacob deceived Isaac into thinking he was Esau. Jacob effectively stole the blessing from his brother, and Esau was not happy about it. In fact, he vowed to kill Jacob. Fearing for his life, Jacob fled from Esau.

Years later, God appeared to Jacob and told him to return home. On his journey, Jacob learned from one of his servants that Esau was up ahead and he had hundreds of armed men with him. Jacob was afraid that Esau would attack him, wipe out his family, and exact his revenge.

On the eve of his encounter with Esau, Jacob was left all alone after sending the others away. He wrestled with God that night. He named the place of his struggle, Peniel, which means "face of God" and then declared "I have seen God face to face and yet my life is preserved."

Jacob emerged from the struggle with his hip dislocated. The next day, he literally crawled and groveled, prostrating himself on the ground in a display of total surrender and submission to his brother. As they approached each other, the Bible reports that Esau ran to his brother, fell on his neck, and kissed him.

Jacob was so relieved and overwhelmed that he offered gifts to his brother, but Esau refused. Jacob said in effect, "Please accept these gifts because **to see your face is like seeing the face of God**—with such favor you have received me." To Jacob, the undeserved forgiveness and mercy was like seeing the face of God.

At the Pile, I experienced the favor, or unmerited grace of God. My face reflected that grace to others.

America suffered a terrible blow on September 11th, 2001. There was much rubble to contend with, but we knew we had to find a way to pick up the pieces and move forward as a nation. At the twentieth anniversary of 9/11, America again seems to be at a crossroads.

During times of national crisis, it is often our political leaders who are tasked with bringing about some measure of unity. President Ronald Reagan was tasked with comforting the nation after the Space Shuttle *Challenger* disaster. Concluding one of the most moving messages in modern presidential history, he stated, "The crew of the Space Shuttle *Challenger* honored us by the way in which they lived their lives. We will never forget them, nor the last time we saw them this morning, as they prepared for the journey and waved goodbye and slipped the surly bonds of earth to touch the face of God."

As a nation and as individuals, we somehow need to slip the surly bonds of earth and touch the face of God. I would humbly suggest that the journey begins with an acknowledgment that we need the grace of God—a grace that He freely offers to us all. Once we are forgiven of our sins and in right relationship with the God who created us, things won't always make sense, but we can find peace in the midst of suffering.

THE TRUE FACE OF GOD

Years ago, I used to share an illustration about a man and his young son. The man was reading the newspaper and his son kept interrupting him. The dad took a page from the newspaper, tore it to pieces, and gave it to his son. "It's a puzzle," he said, assuming it would preoccupy the boy for a while.

After an unusually short time, the boy exclaimed, "Done!"

The dad asked, "How did you do it so quickly?"

"It was easy," the boy replied. "There was a big picture of

a man on one side and a picture of a globe on the other. Once you put the man together right, the world comes together just like that!"

Whatever rubble there is in your life, whatever you have suffered, dear reader, I offer this simple thought. When you picture God, is His face stern? Is it angry?

Maybe, just maybe, God's face toward you is filled with love and compassion. And maybe He longs for you to see Him as He truly is.

> The LORD bless you
> and keep you;
> the LORD make his face shine on you
> and be gracious to you;
> the LORD turn his face toward you
> and give you peace.
>
> — NUMBERS 6:24-26 NIV

NOTES

2. THE CHIRPS OF GROUND ZERO

1. Timothy A. Clary, "First Responders and Volunteers at Ground Zero," updated 9/5/2019, history.com, https://www.history.com/topics/21st-century/ground-zero
2. Ibid
3. thefreedictionary.com, https://www.thefreedictionary.com/jeremiad

3. A DARKNESS THAT COULD BE FELT

1. J. Gilmore Childers and Henry J. DePippo, Senate Judiciary Committee Hearings: "Foreign Terrorists in America: Five Years After the World Trade Center," 2/24/1998, web.archive.org, https://web.archive.org/web/20071227065444/http://judiciary.senate.gov/oldsite/childers.htm
2. Ibid
3. Peter M Leschak, "The JFK assassination: The day the data deluge began," 10/26/2013, startribune.com, https://www.startribune.com/the-jfk-assassination-the-day-the-data-deluge-began/229327621/
4. Jim Dwyer, "Pieces of Bone are Found on Building at 9/11 Site," 4/6/2006, nytimes.com, https://www.nytimes.com/2006/04/06/nyregion/pieces-of-bone-are-found-on-building-at-911-site.html

5. FRESH KILLS

1. "Ground Zero", exhibitions.nysm.nysed.gov, https://exhibitions.nysm.nysed.gov/wtc/recovery/groundzero.html
2. "Richard Marx," servicetoamericanmedals.org, https://servicetoamericamedals.org/honorees/richard-marx/
3. Ibid
4. "A Nation Challenged: The Landfill; At Landfill, Tons of Debris, Slivers of Solace," nytimes.com, https://www.nytimes.-

com/2001/10/21/nyregion/a-nation-challenged-the-landfill-at-landfill-tons-of-debris-slivers-of-solace.html

6. THAT WHICH CAN BE SHAKEN

1. Samantha K. Smith, "Don't Call Him a Hero", 9/8/2016, slate.com, https://slate.com/human-interest/2016/09/dont-call-9-11-first-responders-heroes.html
2. "The Sorting Process," exhibitions.nysm.nysed.gov, https://exhibitions.nysm.nysed.gov/wtc/recovery/sortingprocess.html

7. A LOT WORSE THINGS THAN DYING

1. Larry McShane, "Forensic pathologist details grim work helping identify bodies after 9/11 in new book," 7/19/2014, nydailynews.com, https://www.nydailynews.com/news/national/doctor-details-grim-work-identifying-9-11-bodies-new-book-article-1.1873374
2. Ibid
3. Ibid
4. "Mr Rogers handling the assassination of Robert F Kennedy in 1968" 10/25/2020, facebook.com, https://www.facebook.com/watch/?v=1234949626887808
5. Sara Kettler, "How Mr. Rogers Helped Heal the Nation After Sept. 11th Biography," April 9, 2019
6. "DMORT," web.archive.org, https://web.archive.org/web/20060906150942/http://oep-ndms.dhhs.gov/dmort.html

8. GRIEVING AT THE PIER

1. "CEO Howard Lutnick Remembers Sept. 11: How His Company Survived After Great Personal Loss," 9/11/2016, npr.org, https://www.npr.org/2016/09/11/493491879/ceo-howard-lutnick-remembers-sept-11-how-his-company-survived-after-great-person

9. GOD'S COMFORT

1. Frank T. Shane, "K-9 Disaster Relief," k-9disasterrelief.org, https://www.k-9disasterrelief.org/presentations/
2. Sara Kugler, "Dog Provides Therapy at Ground Zero," 5/20/2016, mrt.com, https://www.mrt.com/news/article/Dog-Provides-Therapy-at-Ground-Zero-7807239.php
3. "5 Famous Small Dogs in History," animalplanet.com, http://www.animalplanet.com/pets/1-smoky-the-wwii-mascot/
4. Mara Bovsun, "The Legacy of 9/11 Dogs," 9/8/2020, akc.org, https://www.akc.org/expert-advice/news/thc-legacy-of-9-11-dogs-18-years-later/
5. Ibid
6. Thom Zones, azquotes.com, https://www.azquotes.com/quote/670899 Accessed 5-25-21

11. THE CROSS IN THE PILE

1. Andrea Morris, "'We Are Standing for the Cross':Christians Unite as Antifa Activists Threaten to Tear Down Cross at Private College," 8/3/2020, 1.cbn.com, https://www1.cbn.com/cbnnews/us/2020/august/we-are-standing-for-the-cross-christians-unite-as-antifa-activists-threaten-to-tear-down-cross-at-private-college
2. Ibid
3. https://latimesblogs.latimes.com/washington/2009/04/obama-notre-dame-georgetown.html
4. Frank Silecchia, "The Cross at Ground Zero," 10/28/2008, guideposts.org, https://www.guideposts.org/inspiration/miracles/gods-grace/the-cross-at-ground-zero
5. Ibid
6. "There's Room at the Cross for You" hymn lyrics by Ira Stanphil

12. I HAVE SEEN THE ENEMY

1. "Sheikh Omar Abdul Rahman Brigade," trackingterrorism.org, https://www.trackingterrorism.org/group/sheikh-omar-abdul-rahman-brigade
2. Saul Alinsky, "Rules for Radicals," Random House, New York, 1971.

3. Paul Kengor, "Saul Alinsky: Playing Merry Hell," 10/13/2020, crisismagazine.com, https://www.crisismagazine.com/2020/saul-alinsky-playing-merry-hell

4. Walt Kelly, "We Have Met the Enemy and He Is Us," 4/22/1971, library.osu.edu, https://library.osu.edu/site/40stories/2020/01/05/we-have-met-the-enemy/

13. RESHAPED FOR A PURPOSE

1. "What happened to the remnants of the World Trade Center?," 9/10/2016, pbs.org, https://www.pbs.org/newshour/nation/happened-remnants-world-trade-center

2. Mary Reed, "*USS New York*: A Ship Forged From Tragedy," 6/11/2007, constructionequipmentguide.com, https://www.constructionequipment-guide.com/uss-new-york-a-ship-forged-from-tragedy/8785

ABOUT THE AUTHOR

 Jim Jenkins was a Navy Reserve Chaplain for 21 years, and a pastor for 40 years. He holds a Doctorate in Ministry from Fuller Theological Seminary, and taught Bible College and Seminary courses at The King's Seminary for more than 10 years. As part of the Chaplain's Emergency Response Team, Jim and the other chaplains received the Distinguished Service Award for their service at Ground Zero. Jim's first book, *Fatal Drift,* was released in 2014. He lives in Monmouth, Oregon, with his wife Judy. They have two children, Hannah and Peter, and five grandchildren. Jim often travels the country to encourage pastors and congregations. He writes a blog found at Jude3Fellowship.com. He is available for speaking engagements and may be reached at chap4sq@msn.com.

RECENT RELEASES

CALLED WRITERS
CHRISTIAN PUBLISHING

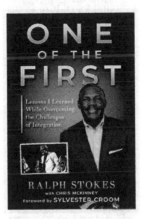

DON'T DO ANYTHING STUPID

A WHITE MAN'S GUIDE TO RACIAL HARMONY

JOHN COVINGTON

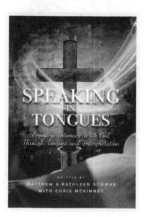

THE
Jericho
FAST

How to Break through Walls
with Prayer and Fasting

RHODA FAYE DIEHL

SPEAKING
IN
TONGUES

*Enjoying Intimacy With God
Through Tongues and Interpretation*

WRITTEN BY
MATTHEW & KATHLEEN SCHWAB
WITH CHRIS MCKINNEY

PUBLISHER'S NOTE: AN INVITATION TO PARADISE

CALLED WRITERS
CHRISTIAN PUBLISHING

All of us wonder why there is pain in the world. We struggle with questions like, "Why would a good God allow so much suffering?" When we ask that question, what we're effectively saying is, "Why doesn't God do something?" We struggle to understand why He doesn't step in and put an end to human suffering once and for all.

The reality is, He is going to do that very thing. One day, He will physically step back into the scene. He is going to put His foot on the Mount of Olives in Jerusalem, and begin the process of restoring earth to its former glory and perfection. The Bible describes the future earth this way:

> *Then I saw "a new heaven and a new earth," for the first heaven and the first earth had passed away, and there was no longer any sea. I saw the Holy City, the new Jerusalem, coming down out of heaven from God, prepared as a bride beautifully dressed for her husband. And I heard a loud voice from the throne*

saying, "Look! God's dwelling place is now among the people, and he will dwell with them. They will be his people, and God himself will be with them and be their God. 'He will wipe every tear from their eyes. There will be no more death' or mourning or crying or pain, for the old order of things has passed away."

He who was seated on the throne said, "I am making everything new!"

— REVELATION 21:1-5 NIV

No more tears. No more pain.

The world that we all long for is coming.

It's on the way.

The big question is: Will you be part of that new world?

In order to be part of that new world, we must receive Jesus Christ as Lord and Savior. There will be pleasures beyond anything we can imagine in that new world. In fact, one of the first things we will experience there is a huge party called, "The Wedding Feast of the Lamb." There will be wine, music, dancing, celebration, and immense joy.

But there will not be any rebellion against God.

The only people who will be in God's new world will be the ones who chose to love Him and give their lives to Him. Just like Jesus asked His disciples, "Who do you say that I am?" we must all answer that same question.

WHO IS JESUS?

God the Father sent His One and Only Son, Jesus Christ, to this imperfect world to redeem us and restore us into a free and open relationship with Himself. Because humankind had sinned, our relationship with God was broken. Severed. And we were under the penalty of sin, which is punishment and death.

Instead of leaving us to suffer those penalties, Jesus decided to take our place. He took our punishment for us by dying a gruesome death on the cross. Jesus was then buried, and on the third day, He was resurrected into eternal life. He defeated death and the grave, and that means we can now freely receive forgiveness for all of our sins.

GOD'S OFFER TO EVERYONE

Eternal life with God in His perfect world is offered to all of us.

If we choose to reject this offer, that means we are choosing sin over God. We are choosing to stay in rebellion toward Him. This will be the result for those who choose to stay in rebellion toward God:

"But the cowardly, the unbelieving, the vile, the murderers, the sexually immoral, those who practice magic arts, the idolaters and all liars—they will be consigned to the fiery lake of burning sulfur. This is the second death."

— REVELATION 21:8 NIV

When presented with options in life, we all want to make the best decision. We weigh all of our important decisions, and we choose carefully.

You can make the right choice today. At this very moment, you are being given the option to end your rebellion toward God, turn away from sin, and choose to receive His forgiveness. You can choose right now to receive Christ as Savior.

A PRAYER FOR SALVATION

If you want to receive Christ as Savior, here is a prayer you can pray right now:

God, I want to live in Heaven with You forever. I do not want to live in sin and rebellion. No human being is perfect, including me. I have done things that You say are wrong. Please forgive me of all my sins, and please give me a new life with You. I now receive Jesus Christ as my Lord and Savior.

Thank you, God, for saving me!

This section of the book is a note from the publisher to share the Gospel of Jesus Christ and invite you, the reader, into a relationship with Him. The reason for this invitation is simple: We want every human being alive to go to Heaven. If you made a decision to receive Christ as Savior today, please reach out to us at CalledWriters.com and let us know.

We want to celebrate with you, and also help you with next steps. God bless you!

ACKNOWLEDGMENTS

Acknowledgements

I would like to express my deep appreciation to the following people:

The U.S. Navy Chaplains Emergency Response Team

Admiral Barry Black, Chief of Chaplains

Captain Leroy Gilbert, Chaplain of the Coast Guard

Captain Wilbur Douglas, Commanding Officer of our team of chaplains at Ground Zero

Admiral Greg Todd, whose immediate response and continual stellar service in New York set the bar high for those of us who came alongside to help.

Admiral Darold Bigger, himself a first responder at the Pentagon on 9/11, who took time to read my manuscript and offer keen insights and much needed encouragement.

Admiral Endel Lee, whose example and steady modeling of discipline and pastoral care helped me to be a better chaplain.

Captain Ray Houck, my colleague, and my friend. Thank

you for looking at my manuscript and for your exemplary career serving our country, and our Lord.

Captain Barry Crane, who had the presence of mind and dedication to take on the role of historian and chronicler of the Navy Chaplain Corps response to 9/11.

Chaplain Denny Boyle. Our paths crossed numerous times during our careers. Your quiet behind-the-scenes pastoral care to those affected by the TWA Flight 800 disaster, the tragic death of JFK Jr., and to those devasted by the events of 9/11, revealed your servant's heart. Your humble willingness to serve out of the limelight and your devotion to God represent the best practices for all who wear the uniform and bear the title of Chaplain. First on scene, invisible to all but our Lord. Serving with you has been a singular honor and privilege.

The congregation of the Cottage Grove Faith Center, Cottage Grove Oregon. Our 20 years together was quite a ride. Thank you for putting up with my absences, and my preoccupation with first responders and veterans. You allowed me to have a broad reach, and, in many ways, it was your graciousness that made my ministry effective.

Sandy Silverthorne, award-winning author, actor, pastor, and trusted friend. Your input was invaluable as I wrote this book. Your books have, and will continue to have, a huge impact on the next generation. I think I'd like to be more like you when I grow up.

Cheryl Links, award-winning photographer. Your keen eye, and artistic skill made me look presentable for the cover —no small accomplishment.

Greg Hinnant, author, pastor, and passionate contender for the faith. Your editorial instincts and willingness to offer correction and suggestions for improvement helped me finish this book.

Chris Dalton and Nathan Dalton. The Lord brought you into my life at exactly the right time to encourage me to keep writing.

Chris and Shannon McKinney, the whole team at Called Writers, and publicist Laura Douglass. It could not have been easy to deal with someone who is primarily a preacher masquerading as a writer. Working with you has been a pleasure.

Finally, to His Honor the Mayor of New York City, Rudy Giuliani. Your leadership during the nightmare that was 9/11 rivaled that of Winston Churchill during the bombing of London. I saw you everywhere. You personally attended hundreds of first responders' funerals, gave countless interviews, and endured unfair criticism; all the while dealing with your own loss and grief as you led an army of assets from around the world. I took a ferry boat ride with you that I will never forget.

Made in the USA
Middletown, DE
21 September 2021